D0117510

Teacher Study Groups

NCTE Editorial Board: Pat Cordeiro, Bobbi Fisher, Xin Liu Gale, Sarah Hudelson, Bill McBride, Alleen Pace Nilsen, Helen Poole, Jerrie Cobb Scott, Karen Smith, Chair, ex officio, Peter Feely, ex officio

Teacher Study Groups

Building Community through Dialogue and Reflection

Barb Birchak, Clay Connor,
Kathleen Marie Crawford, Leslie H. Kahn,
Sandy Kaser, Susan Turner,
and
Kathy G. Short

National Council of Teachers of English
1111 W. Kenyon Road, Urbana, Illinois 61801-1096

Staff Editor: Zarina M. Hock

Interior Design: Doug Burnett and Carlton Bruett

Cover Design: Loren Kirkwood

NCTE Stock Number: 48468-3050

©1998 by the National Council of Teachers of English. All rights reserved. Printed in the United States of America.

It is the policy of NCTE in its journals and other publications to provide a forum for the open discussion of ideas concerning the content and the teaching of English and the language arts. Publicity accorded to any particular point of view does not imply endorsement by the Executive Committee, the Board of Directors, or the membership at large, except in announcements of policy, where such endorsement is clearly specified.

Library of Congress Cataloging-in-Publication Data

Teacher study groups: building community through dialogue and reflection/
    Barb Birchak . . . [et al.].
        p.   cm.
    Includes bibliographical references.
    ISBN 0-8141-4846-8 (pbk.)
    1. Teacher work groups—United States. 2. Teachers—In-service
training—United States. I. Birchak, Barb, 1942–   . II. National Council
of Teachers of English.
LB1731.T4196 1998
370'.071'55—dc21   98-38170
                                                                        CIP

To our colleagues who share our journey as we build community through dialogue and reflection

Contents

Acknowledgments

There are many people who supported us professionally and personally as we worked on this project. We first want to acknowledge the children in our classrooms who think with us and who constantly challenge our assumptions about their potentials as learners. They motivate and inspire us to continue our own learning and to move out of our isolation to build relationships with colleagues.

We want to thank Rebecca Montaño, Myna Matlin, and Virginia Romero, who appreciated the study group as a new vision for professional development and provided encouragement and administrative support within the Tucson Unified School District. We are likewise grateful to Rosanna Gallagher and Mary Belle Mitchell for sustaining that vision when members of the group moved to new schools.

We are deeply indebted to all of those who actually participated in the study groups. While their names have been changed to protect their identities, their voices provide the context, the "warp" through which we weave our interpretations. Their insights helped us identify the patterns that emerge when teachers build community through dialogue and reflection with each other.

We also want to acknowledge the University of Arizona Foundation and the Office of the Vice President of Research for a Small Grant, the International Reading Association for an Elva Knight Research Grant, and the National Council of Teachers of English for a Grant-in-Aid. These grants provided us with financial support to gather and analyze data from the teacher study groups.

Two members of our research team, Pamella Sherman and Charlene Klassen, were unable to work with us on the writing of this book, but played important roles in the data analysis. Thanks also to Gloria Kauffman and LaFon Phillips, who lent their skills as photographers; Sharon Alexandra, who painstakingly transcribed our tapes; and Stacie Cook Emert, Barbara Bernard, Gloria Kauffman, Jean Schroeder, and the other reviewers, who read and responded to our early drafts.

And finally, we thank the significant others in our lives who respected our need to write, suffered through the inconveniences of eating late or alone, and assumed a little more than their share of responsibilities. Our thanks and love go to Becky, Russell, Nancy, Susan, Lucy, Lynn, Margie, Carl, Jerry, and to Sam the Cat, who so graciously and sometimes not so graciously tolerated our invasion of his domain.

1 Why Form a Teacher Study Group?

As teachers, we have experienced how difficult it is to find time to reflect on our teaching or to engage in a meaningful conversation with a colleague. We race from meeting to meeting, from student to student, and from one crisis to another. And that's all in the course of a *normal* day.

Our interest in study groups developed out of a growing need to talk with colleagues about professional issues—to stop running past each other in hallways and to actually take time to reflect and dialogue about teaching and learning. We would see each other in faculty meetings, child study sessions, and various school committees, but these meetings had particular agendas with specific items of business. We were incredibly alone in a school full of people. While it would seem natural for schools to be places where educators come together and share professional concerns, we had experienced only occasional collaboration with one or two colleagues.

We began to raise questions about establishing a community of educators within a school. Could we find a way to make reflection and dialogue part of our daily lives as professionals in schools? Was it possible to slow down long enough to think about how we "did" school? Could we productively talk about our differences as teachers and find ways to use those differences to build a stronger school? How could our voices as teachers become a stronger part of the curricular changes within the school and across the district? Were there other approaches to professional development beyond the one day "shot-in-the-arm" inservice that introduced a new approach by the newest expert?

These concerns led us to search for a form of professional development that recognized our voices as professionals and provided long-term support for reflection and dialogue. We became interested in teacher study groups and worked with our school district to form groups in the schools where we were teaching. While the basic format of study groups is simple and straightforward, personal experience tells us that successfully organizing and maintaining a study group can be complex and difficult. Human relationships are never simple, especially when the dialogue is about questions and topics that matter to us professionally.

As we wrote this book, we wanted to highlight the issues involved in starting and maintaining a teacher study group. We decided to include many practical suggestions for organizing, facilitating, and dealing with group dynamics within a study group. We also realized, however, that our suggestions grow out of our particular experiences in our individual school settings. Because each school and community has its own context, study groups necessarily will vary in how they are organized and in the issues they face. In this chapter, we share the issues and school contexts that led us to teacher study groups and the groups in which we have been involved.

How Our Study Group Got Started

A number of years ago, the Tucson Unified School District moved from a traditional basal approach to the use of literature anthologies and sets of trade books as part of the textbook- adoption cycle for reading instruction. This shift reflected a broader district focus on interactive approaches to learning, in which students are actively and meaningfully engaged as learners in high-level academic tasks and thinking. Teachers throughout the district viewed this move as a challenging one. Some responded with excitement and a feeling of validation for what they were doing in their classrooms, while other teachers viewed the change with uncertainty and fear; still others responded with a "wait-and-see" attitude. Because of district finances, only two half-day workshops on literature-based curriculum were offered to teachers in the seventy-three elementary schools. Murmurs of frustration and tension built across the district.

Because Kathy Short was teaching children's literature and curriculum at the University of Arizona, she frequently received calls to provide short inservices in various schools. Kathy had been feeling uncomfortable about this type of inservice for some time, and the district move to literature-based curriculum brought her nagging questions to the forefront. It bothered her that while curricular reforms were aimed at putting children at the center of their learning, the inservices offered to teachers continued to be dominated by transmission models of learning.

As an elementary teacher, Kathy had not found inservices to be productive, primarily because teachers in her school were not given a voice in their focus. Even when an inservice or conference excited her, her enthusiasm waned once the demands of thirty children and a frantic schedule hit. She would give the idea a try but would drop it if the idea didn't work immediately. There was no time to reflect, nor was there a group of teachers with whom to talk. Creating curriculum with students had never occurred to her. Curriculum was something that came from experts outside the classroom, and so she engaged in an unending search for new experts to consult and new programs to implement.

When she became a teacher educator, Kathy taught university courses, presented at conferences, and conducted inservices and workshops in school settings. She worked closely with schools to ensure that these inservices were not isolated presentations, but part of ongoing professional development in which teachers had a strong voice. She changed her courses so that curriculum was negotiated and teachers were actively engaged in reflecting on their learning with each other. However, while these courses, conferences, and inservices provided alternative perspectives and practices for educators to consider, she felt frustrated that they did not support day-to-day work in schools.

A major concern was the lack of long-term, continuing professional development that enables teachers to establish their own agenda. Through her work with children, Kathy had come to value the power of dialogue and reflection. She recognized that children need time to pull back from their actions and reflect in order to take charge of their own learning. It was obvious that most teachers had so little time to think that reflection was a luxury few felt they could afford in the frantic pace of the day.

Another concern was related to the deficit view of teachers and change that underlies most efforts at curriculum reform and professional development. These efforts often focus on determining what is wrong with teachers and then offering a program to "fix" their teaching. Change is not viewed as a natural part of learning and professional growth. Nor are teachers seen as capable of transforming themselves (Lester & Onore, 1990). Instead, whenever there are problems in schools, it is assumed that the problems are teachers and their teaching strategies. There is no recognition that many of these problems are inherent in the social and institutional structures of the broader society.

What makes this attitude even more problematic is that research clearly indicates that curriculum reform fails unless teachers are involved in defining their own problems, creating knowledge, and transforming themselves to help bring about educational change (Fullan & Stiegelbauer, 1991; Lieberman & Miller, 1991). Instead of prescriptive mandates or packaged programs, teachers need time to work with each other to think, analyze, and create conditions for change in their specific circumstances and in ways that fit their own needs (Cochran-Smith & Lytle, 1990). However, these recommendations for dialogue are not easy to implement within the realities of daily schedules. Where in the crowded, fast-paced life of classrooms and schools are teachers to find time to reflect and dialogue together?

While the potential exists for a community of teachers to form within individual schools, Kathy had not as yet experienced this kind of professional support in schools. At best, teachers had positive social relationships, but discussions about teaching were usually avoided because of theoretical and curricular differences and the lack of time. Kathy had been part of TAWL (Teachers Applying Whole Language) groups where teachers from different schools who shared common theoretical views and interests met to learn together through talking and reading. Since these groups had played a powerful role in her own thinking, she wondered whether it was possible to form this same kind of support network within a school despite the theoretical and personal differences that separate teachers.

After hearing Elizabeth Saavedra and Luis Moll talk about their work with teacher study groups as part of a large research project on funds of knowledge in Latino households (Moll, 1992), Kathy was further convinced of the effectiveness of study groups. School-based study groups seemed to provide the context needed for critical dialogue about issues of learning and teaching. They did not begin with a specific agenda or plan of professional development but with a focus on negotiating a shared agenda and encouraging professional growth. Teachers could take a step back from their practice and beliefs and, in a supportive environment, critique those practices and beliefs by knowledge gained through the study group process.

Knowing that the only way to understand the potential of study groups was to become involved in one, Kathy took a proposal to establish a school-based study group to Rebecca Montaño, Assistant Superintendent of Curriculum, Instruction, and Student Learning, in the Tucson Unified School District. Through Montaño's efforts, several schools were contacted, and the principals of several schools responded. Warren Elementary School was selected as the site of the project, and teachers from a neighboring school, Maldonado Elementary School, were also invited. While Kathy could have gone directly to schools to inquire about starting a study group, she worked through the district office so that the project would have a greater chance of becoming part of the district system. She knew from past experiences that university-school collaborations which remain outside district structures tend to have short lives that are dependent on university participation.

After meeting with the two principals, Myna Matlin and Virginia Romero, to discuss the logistical issues of a teacher study group, Kathy attended a regular faculty meeting at each school and introduced the concept of a study group. The study group was presented as a voluntary group of teachers who would meet right after school dismissal for an hour-and-a-half every other week to talk about their issues and concerns related to the broad topic of literature-based curriculum. The focus of the group would be for them to dialogue and reflect with each other rather than listen to presentations, and Kathy's role would be to facilitate those discussions. After this brief explanation, the first date for the study group meeting was announced and anyone who was interested was invited to attend.

The initial meetings were attended by classroom teachers, the librarian, the principal, resource teachers, and student teachers. About two-thirds of the staff at Warren joined the group and five teachers from Maldonado. Their reasons for joining the group were quite diverse. Some joined out of an interest in study groups and in dialogue with other teachers, while others wanted to learn more about literature-based curriculum. Several joined because they had heard Kathy present at inservices and valued her expertise. Some felt a strong need for more community in the school among staff members. While they weren't necessarily sure they would benefit professionally from the group, they wanted to support other teachers. Others joined because they were encouraged by peers or had a friend in the group. Still others came because they hoped to influence the thinking of other teachers in the building. Some came because they wanted to know what was happening and did not want to be left out of any power networks that might form. Several came because they had received negative evaluations from the principal and felt that they needed to be present. A few joined because they could get university credit. Many were unsure what the group would actually be or whether it would really be worth their time. Most assumed it would be a form of inservice where Kathy would share ideas and they would then discuss those ideas.

At the first meeting, the members of the group brainstormed a list of issues that concerned us as we considered the move toward literature-based curriculum. At the end of that meeting, we looked back over the lists we had created and talked about which issue we wanted to start with at the following meeting. We started the next meeting with sharing, then talked about the issue that was our focus that afternoon, and ended with a short discussion on what we wanted to talk about next. This structure of general sharing, focused dialogue, and negotiation of our next focus worked well for us, and we continued to follow this structure in subsequent meetings. Depending on the focus, we would decide whether to do some professional reading or to try something in our classroom settings before we met.

This format supported conversation and dialogue among group members and changed their perceptions about study groups and why they would want to be members of such a group. There was frustration at first because some felt that Kathy was holding back on them, and they wanted her to share more of her ideas. Over time, however, members of the group realized that this meeting was a form of professional development in which they were responsible for sharing and thinking together, not an occasion to come and hear a presentation. Initially, however, not everyone was convinced that the study group would be a worthwhile experience.

In writing this book, we reflected on why we decided to stay in the group despite our feelings of uncertainty at the start. Clay Connor noted that it was a support group of colleagues who were willing to "push the envelope" of their thinking. He was able to take ideas from the study group to help his students learn in ways that were meaningful, challenging, and interesting. He felt that the study group brought people together, illuminated important understandings, and dissipated some myths about teaching.

While Sandy Kaser joined the group for the literature focus, she came to value the dialogue that was taking place. Having a regular time to talk and think together became so important to her that she now seldom embarks on any major professional task without finding people who will work collaboratively with her.

Kathleen Crawford had found that most university courses did not provide time to think through issues and discuss them with other class members, especially since the class met only once a week. She rarely got to know people well enough to initiate conversations nor did she see them again during the week. In the study group, a sense of community was built, and the conversations about practices and beliefs were carried over into other parts of the school setting and day.

Like Kathleen, Barb Birchak was drawn to the group because she valued dialogue among teachers concerning children's learning. She had also seen Kathy present at several inservices and wanted to work with her. Once she became involved in the group, she grew professionally in her thinking about her own classroom and in her relationships with other teachers in ways she had not anticipated.

Leslie Kahn initially did not value the process of thinking together because she had never been involved in such a group. She joined hesitantly because her real interest was mathematics, not literature. Over time she came to value the process of discussing issues and ideas relevant to her classroom. She found herself becoming more articulate about what she thought, and she felt accepted and supported as well as questioned and challenged.

Susan Turner's initial interest was in learning about literature-based reading programs and implementing children's discussion groups. She expected a transmission model where Kathy would impart knowledge, but found that the study group departed from this model and recognized everyone as experts. The structure of the study group with its rotation of roles required every participant to look at each member differently and gave teachers the opportunity to talk with each other as professionals. This experience convinced Susan that she did not want to return to being a passive participant in her own growth. For all of us, this group was a place where we truly felt "professional" and to be treated as anything less than that was unacceptable.

How Did Our Study Groups Develop over Time?

This section presents an overview of the history of our involvement with school-based study groups over the last seven years. These groups made major changes over those periods of time and transformed themselves in different ways. Some years have been more productive and successful than others, but we have learned from all of these experiences. In later sections we will be sharing specific examples and insights from these groups.

The Warren Study Group

The Warren/Maldonado study group met the first year in the Warren school library to discuss the use of literature in response to the district's move towards a literature-based curriculum. Kathy was the facilitator of the group. She also visited in classrooms at both schools every other week to give teachers additional support. In our study group sessions, we shared literature experiences from our classrooms, talked about the theoretical and practical basis of literature-based curriculum, and read professional articles.

During the second year, the study group shifted to an emphasis on evaluation and portfolios, again in response to district-initiated changes. The study group became very large and so, in January, the Maldonado group began their own study group at their school. Kathy continued to facilitate the Warren group, which moved into discussing classroom management.

History of Study Groups.

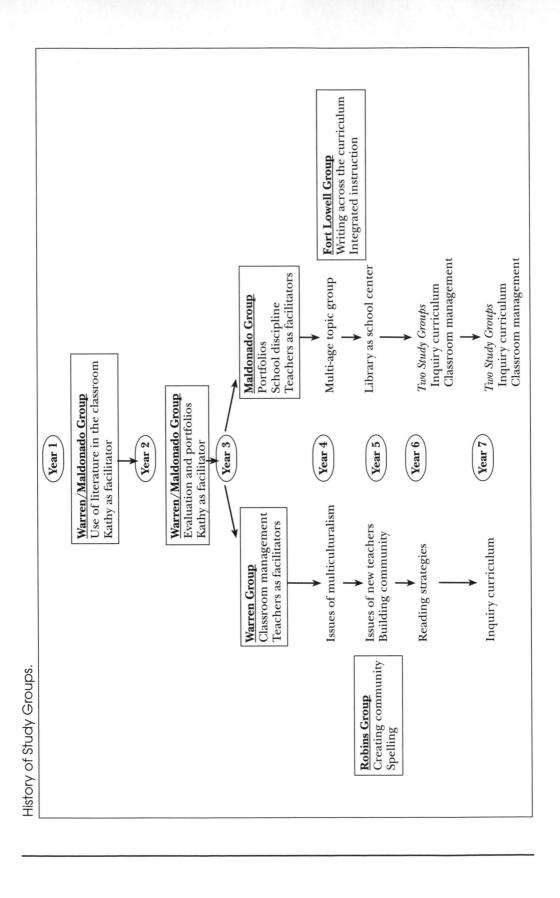

The third year of the Warren group began with looking at issues of culture through reading and discussing adult novels from diverse cultures as an adult-readers group. Due to a district move away from mathematics textbooks, the group then spent the second half of the year discussing mathematics. Teachers from within the study group served as the facilitators. An additional development was the opportunity to visit in each others' classrooms or to visit other schools. The principal brought in a substitute teacher one day a week so that each teacher had an opportunity to visit someone else.

During the fourth year of the group, a school committee of three people was formed to organize the study group sessions. Since the school was organized around a committee structure, this new committee signaled that the study group had become part of the school structure, not a special event. Much of the discussion that year was on issues of multiculturalism.

During the fifth year of the group, Warren became a bilingual school and so there were many new teachers in the building. Many different topics, such as portfolios and literature circles, were discussed as teachers got to know one another. During the second part of the year, the group read *Life in a Crowded Place* (Peterson, 1992) and discussed building community and establishing caring and trust in classrooms.

Because Warren began the sixth year with a new principal who didn't know the school's history, the study group committee and the study group were not initially part of the school structure. In late September, the teachers initiated the group themselves through an announcement at a faculty meeting. Because most members were primary teachers, the initial sessions focused on reading strategies and later moved to issues of democracy and inquiry. A small group continued during the seventh year to talk about inquiry and read *Learning Together through Inquiry* (Short, Schroeder, Laird, Kauffman, Ferguson, & Crawford, 1996).

The Maldonado Study Group

The Maldonado group split off from the combined group during the second year and formed their own group for several reasons. One was that the large size of the group made sharing and discussion more difficult to meet the needs of the members. The second was that Maldonado wanted to develop the same sense of community in their own school which they saw forming at Warren. The group continued the discussion of portfolios and then talked about school discipline using the book *Discipline with Dignity* (Curwin & Mendler, 1988) and worked on a student handbook for the school. Various members took turns serving as facilitator. The principal also established a teacher-to-teacher program one day a week where a substitute teacher released teachers to visit each other's classrooms.

The Maldonado group began the third year with a large group of teachers. Because the district had adopted a new mathematics program, the group took this topic on as a focus. As interest in this topic waned, so did attendance at the meetings and so the group changed directions and looked at the teaching of writing.

During the fourth year, Maldonado started a multi-age strand in the school and teachers who were involved with, or interested in, multi-age teaching formed a study group. This group was topic-centered and was not a schoolwide group. The following year, one teacher took on the responsibility of offering the study group as an option in the school. The primary focus of the group was on the library as the center of the school.

In the sixth and seventh years, several study groups operated in the school. One small group of five met to discuss issues relevant to multi-age classrooms, inquiry, and literature-based reading strategies. The group alternated between discussing readings from *Creating Classrooms for Authors and Inquirers* (Short & Harste, 1996) and talking about experiences in their classrooms. Another group formed around discussions of classroom management and discipline.

Our Participation in Other Study Groups

In addition to the Warren and Maldonado study groups, we have been part of several other study groups which we will reference throughout this book. At the end of the first year, Myna Matlin, the principal at Warren, talked with Kathy about the important role the study group was playing in creating a sense of professional community in that school. Myna commented that while she was benefiting greatly from this study group, she had no place where she could talk with peers about her needs and concerns as a principal. She felt isolated, rarely seeing other principals. When principals did meet, these meetings were about new procedures, bus routes, and test scores. There wasn't time for meaningful dialogue with colleagues. Her concerns led to the formation of a principal study group which began meeting the following year and is still meeting six years later. This group usually meets from 7:30–9:15 a.m. two to three times a month from January through April in a school that is centrally located in the city. The membership changes slightly each year, varying from fifteen to twenty principals. Kathy serves as co-facilitator of this group with Rebecca Montaño, a district central administrator.

As is normal in a large school district, a number of us have changed schools and become involved in study groups in our new contexts. Clay moved to Fort Lowell Elementary School and was asked to provide a teacher inservice on writing across the curriculum. He concluded the inservice with an invitation to form a long-term study group to continue discussion of this issue along with other curricular concerns. He applied for district inservice credit so teachers could receive district recognition for their participation in the group.

For the first two years, Clay served as the organizer and facilitator of the group. A wide range of topics were discussed including writing, curriculum articulation, professional resources at the school, literature, inquiry, and a model of integrated instruction. When Clay was unable to continue, other teachers took on the role of facilitator and formed study groups on topics of concern to the school.

Sandy and Leslie moved to Robins Elementary School, a brand-new school in the district. The teachers and students came from many different buildings. Establishing community was critical at all levels. Kathy was asked to work with the teachers in a combination study group/ inservice format that focused around reading *Life in a Crowded Place* (Peterson, 1992) and discussing ways to establish community with children, parents, and each other. The study group met once a month on an early-release day. Usually half of the time was spent in a study group discussion format and the other half in a workshop format.

After having no study group for a year, Leslie and Sandy took the lead and proposed a study group focused on the topic of spelling. This voluntary group met every other week to read and discuss journal articles on spelling from the National Council of Teachers of English. Teachers also engaged in teacher research in their classrooms as they tried out engagements with students and shared these with the group. Three teachers, including Leslie and Sandy, shared the roles of facilitator, notetaker, and organizer for the meetings.

Conclusion

We did not become involved in teacher study groups because we were looking for something to fill our time. We are committed teachers who were already putting a lot of time and thought into our teaching. In fact, if someone had asked us, we would have said it wasn't possible to squeeze anything else into our professional lives. So our initial commitment to the teacher study group was very tentative. If it hadn't been productive, we would have quickly moved away from the group. We have continued to participate because our involvement in these groups adds an important dimension to our teaching and to our relationships with other teachers in our buildings.

We wrote the chapters in this book to answer some of the key questions that we asked ourselves and that others have asked us about the study groups. Chapter 2 focuses on a question that we often asked the first several years—"What *exactly* is a study group?" We wanted to understand how these groups differed from other forms of professional development. This chapter also includes comments from teacher interviews on what was significant about the study group experience for them. Chapter 3 addresses practical decisions related to the question, "How are teacher study groups organized?" We reflect on our experiences starting a group, making logistical decisions, and determining the agenda. Chapter 4 is organized around the question, "How are study groups facilitated?" The role of the facilitator became increasingly important to us in our work with study groups. A related question, "What does a study group session sound like?" is the focus of Chapter 5. This chapter includes an edited transcript from an actual study group session to show the types of talk that occur within the group and the ways in which the facilitator interacts throughout the meeting. As might be expected, there are many potential pitfalls as well as high points in study groups. Chapter 6 examines these through our reflections on the question, "What are the issues that study groups confront?"

The final chapter, Chapter 7, examines the question of "What is the influence of dialogue and reflection beyond the study group?" It includes a discussion of ways groups can incorporate reflection on the study group process through their own teacher research. During the first three years of the Warren and Maldonado groups, we received grant funding from several sources to collect and analyze data from the study groups. The funding did not support the groups themselves, but was used for data collection and analysis. We met in the summers to examine the end-of-the-year interviews and transcripts of the study group sessions. This research allowed us to take a more reflective approach to examining what was and was not working in the groups and was the basis for identifying the issues, suggestions, and examples included in this book.

2 What Is a Study Group?

When we first began our teacher study group, the question "What *exactly* is a study group?" was foremost in our minds. We saw the study group as a place where we could negotiate a shared agenda instead of having someone else's agenda imposed on us. We knew that our focus was on recognizing collaborative dialogue as a way of thinking through our issues and concerns, rather than relying on outside experts. For us, the study group signaled that we were the experts and the best coordinators of our professional growth.

However, as often happens, our theory was ahead of our practice. Although we believed in study groups we were not sure what they would really look like. Because so many of our experiences involved professional development in which outside experts presented to us on their work, we weren't exactly sure what would go on in a study group where there were no presentations.

We did not reject the role of outside experts in our professional growth; instead, we saw them as resources for informing our own deliberations. We believed that we could generate our own knowledge through dialogue as well as reflect on and process the work of other educators. The group was a place where we could explore and develop innovations that came from our questions and interests, rather than relying on mandates and prescriptive approaches. Instead of changing our teaching with each new fad or mandate, we wanted to thoughtfully critique our own beliefs and practices, explore alternative possibilities, and take charge of our own professional journeys.

What Does a Study Group Look like?

In trying to determine what a study group was, one of our first tasks was to develop a structure for our study group sessions. When we began, we weren't even sure what would happen in a session because none of us had previously attended a school-based study group. We had to find a structure that would facilitate thoughtful critique and dialogue in supportive, not destructive, ways. Because the study group existed to meet the needs of its members and their professional growth, the format needed to accommodate their personal growth. As long as the people within the group were responsible for the agenda, there were many possibilities for formats and structures.

Over time, we found a structure that met our needs. We often met for an hour-and-a-half in the school library on Wednesday or Thursday afternoons as soon as school was dismissed. We met on a regular basis, every other week throughout the school year, so that the study groups became part of how we "did school."

Sessions usually began with informal conversations and sharing classroom experiences. We shared exciting events in our lives and classrooms and asked for support as we faced problems and frustrations or hunted for resources. We then moved into discussing our focus for that particular session and talked about theoretical and practical issues related to the focus. We ended each session by talking about our focus for the following meeting and what we would do to prepare for that meeting.

While finding a structure that worked helped us get the group started, we continued to struggle with many issues and kept returning to our question of "What is a study group?" In many cases, we figured out what it was by determining what it wasn't.

A Study Group Is Not a Staff Meeting

We quickly learned that a study group should not become another staff meeting to discuss school policy and business. Because study groups often include the most active members of the staff, many new ideas for school policies are generated in the sessions. As a result, staff members who choose not to attend may be excluded from important decisions. An additional problem is that policy issues begin to dominate the sessions and circumvent thoughtful dialogue about issues.

For example, the Maldonado study group spent several months putting together a student handbook. The study group meetings became work sessions where different group members wrote individual parts of the handbook. This resulted in negative feelings among other faculty members who were not part of the study group because they felt excluded from the process. In addition, study group members became resentful because there was no time to thoughtfully discuss issues of classroom management.

While school policies need to be the focus of staff meetings, not study group sessions, the study group can play a role by brainstorming and developing possible plans of action. For example, the Warren group had a productive discussion about the relationship between parents and schools that resulted in a long list of ways that parents, the local community, and the school might work together. This list of ideas was then taken to a staff meeting where teachers and staff members discussed the actions they wanted to take as a school.

A Study Group Is Not an Inservice

The model of professional development with which we were all most familiar was the inservice, where an educator from the school or a university presented theoretical and practical ideas. Many expected our group to be a variation of an inservice, just with more discussion. It was difficult to value learning from each other through dialogue rather than learning from an "expert." While we struggled with how to engage in productive dialogue, we resisted turning the study group into an inservice where someone from the group presented ideas, recognizing that those opportunities for presentations and inservices already existed in the school; we wanted the study group to provide a different alternative. The study group did not replace these other forms of professional development but added another dimension.

However, we did find that the study group sessions were a good place to identify topics or issues for inservices. When we saw that there was a lack of a common knowledge base from which the group could productively have a discussion, we identified this as an inservice topic. For example, when many questions about reading strategies kept coming up in our study group, Kathy presented an after-school inservice on this topic. The presentation was not part of the study group, but a separate inservice for all of the teachers in the school. During the next study group, we discussed the inservice and processed the ideas for ourselves. When the study group moved into a discussion of mathematics, we found ourselves struggling because we lacked the background to discuss these issues productively and so asked for additional inservice.

While we valued the ideas of experts, we no longer accepted their ideas without question. Instead, their ideas became part of the resources we used in our study group process and dialogue.

In another school, teachers decided to alternate inservices with study group meetings. The teachers in the building had requested professional development on evaluation, for which they decided to meet twice a month. At the first meeting each month, they had an inservice presentation by teacher educators or teachers on some issue of evaluation. This meeting was mandatory for all teachers. Two weeks later, a voluntary study group met so teachers could process the inservice and talk about their ongoing work in their own classrooms related to evaluation.

We have specified what a study group is not. What, then, *is* a study group?

A Study Group

- Requires voluntary commitment
- Builds community and caring
- Challenges our thinking as educators
- Integrates theory and practice

A Study Group Requires Voluntary Commitment

One clarification that immediately became important to us is that a study group is a *voluntary* group of teachers. Initially our group had to be voluntary because we met after school, but as we later interacted in other groups that met on school time, it became apparent that the voluntary nature of the group was essential to its success. In fact, we found that the quickest way to ensure the failure of a group is to mandate attendance. Study groups are based on the belief that teachers need to take charge of their own learning and transformation and this belief is violated when they are forced to attend the group.

Some study groups in other schools have an early release day once a week and so meet during the actual school day. When study groups meet on school time, there is a strong temptation to mandate attendance. We believe that other professional development options need to be available as choices, such as teachers working individually or with a partner on curriculum development, engaging in professional reading, viewing professional videotapes, etc. The issue is one of choice.

A Study Group Builds Community and Challenges Our Thinking

Another realization we came to was that a study group involves multiple purposes, which include building a sense of community and caring as well as challenging beliefs and practice. We gradually came to understand that the two purposes were not in opposition to each other but were both essential to the study group process.

There were times when the study group sessions primarily involved teachers sharing their frustrations. Instead of spending fifteen to twenty minutes sharing "joys and sorrows," the entire session was spent in this sharing, and the group never got to their agreed-upon agenda. Some group members felt that their present situation was so stressful that dialogue about difficult issues was impossible. They argued that in order to create community, they needed time to vent their frustrations and to get to know each other better by sharing. Other group members, however, came to the group to push their thinking about teaching, and they resented spending the entire session sharing.

While we did find that occasionally study group sessions focused on sharing because of district or school crises, for the most part we stayed with our structure of having some sharing and a group focus. By combining the two, the needs of various group members were met, and they had to consider others' needs as well. Group members got to know each other and created a stronger sense of community with each other, but they also thought deeply and critically about their teaching.

A Study Group Integrates Theory and Practice

We also came to see that a study group must integrate theory and practice in powerful ways. Study groups cannot only be places to exchange practical ideas and activities. Without also discussing the "big ideas" that underlie these activities, we found that the activities were of little use, and we quickly tired of the group. There wasn't much to discuss.

Two different groups in which we participated revolved around particular members sharing activities—one on math manipulatives and the other on spelling programs and activities. In both cases, there was little discussion among group members other than requesting clarification on a procedure. Members walked away with a set of activities but no discussion of why they would want to do that activity or sense of how to develop their own classroom engagements.

When our interest in evaluation led us to field notes, we talked about different kinds of field notes and ways to find time to write notes in the classroom. In the midst of this practical discussion, one group member asked, "Why would I even want to take field notes?" Her question stopped the group and led to a generative discussion about the purpose for field notes and the role they play in constructing curriculum that is based on students' own needs and interests.

On the other hand, when we stayed only with theory and didn't talk about ways to bring these ideas into our classrooms, we were frustrated and felt the group wasn't "productive." At one point, we spent several sessions talking about sharing control and collaborating with students to create curriculum. While most could agree theoretically on these issues, the major question became "But what difference does it make in the classroom?" Because of our interest in literature, we looked at literature discussion groups and how we might organize these groups differently if we believed in collaborative curriculum.

The constant movement between theory and practice became an essential aspect of study groups. If we found ourselves focusing on activities, we took time to talk about *why* those ideas supported our overall curriculum or philosophy. If we found that our discussion had stayed at a theoretical level, we pulled back and asked "So what does this mean for our classrooms?"

What Are the Different Types of Study Groups?

Another issue involved in defining study groups was our realization that there are different types of groups and that any of these types can take on a different focus. The major emphasis of this book is on teacher study groups that are *school-based groups*. These groups are composed of educators within a particular school—classroom teachers, resource teachers, the principal, the librarian, student teachers, and classroom assistants. The major focus is on teaching concerns as shared by different members of the school staff. These groups have the advantage of easy accessibility for group members because meetings occur at the school. In addition, these study groups positively influence staff relationships and knowledge of what is happening in other classrooms and parts of the school.

Another type is *job-alike groups* where educators who share a particular position meet to network and discuss issues that arise from their particular responsibilities. Job-alike groups that have been formed include study groups for principals, librarians, curriculum coordinators, and kindergarten teachers. Often the members of these groups do not have others in their school contexts who share their same position and so feel a sense of isolation and a need to talk with someone else who has the same responsibilities.

Topic-centered groups are another type of group. These groups are often composed of teachers from different schools who want to explore a specific issue. Sometimes these study groups are smaller interest groups that are part of organizations such as a TAWL group, a local reading council, or an NCTE affiliate. The membership of these groups can be much broader and may include community members, administrators, and others. Another example is the study groups that NCTE has been supporting, such as the study groups on spelling and reading instruction.

This type of group is usually formed for a shorter period of time and doesn't have the ongoing nature of school-based groups. They form in relation to a current interest or concern and, after a period of time, the group disbands as members move on to new issues. We have been members of study groups on multi-age classrooms, inquiry, and sign systems. These groups often have more difficulty finding a time and place to meet, but they have the advantage of members sharing theoretical beliefs and focusing more deeply on a particular issue.

In these various study groups, different decisions have been made about the focus of the discussion. Most of our school-based study groups

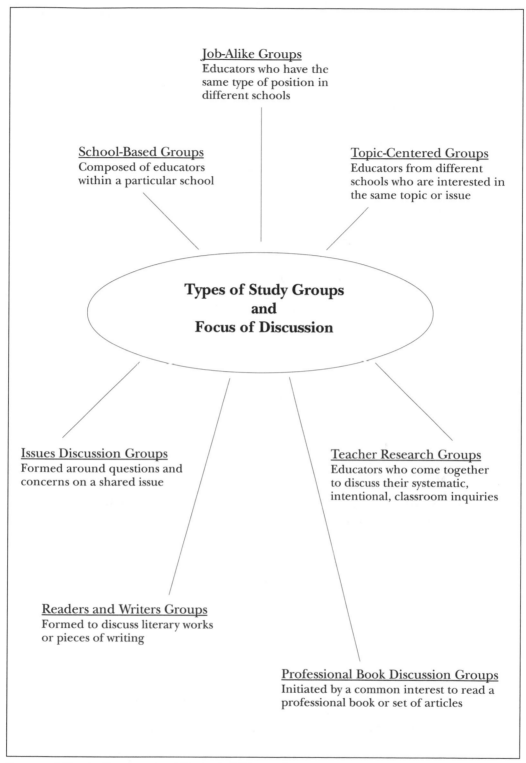

Job-Alike Groups
Educators who have the
same type of position in
different schools

School-Based Groups
Composed of educators
within a particular school

Topic-Centered Groups
Educators from different
schools who are interested in
the same topic or issue

**Types of Study Groups
and
Focus of Discussion**

Issues Discussion Groups
Formed around questions and
concerns on a shared issue

Teacher Research Groups
Educators who come together
to discuss their systematic,
intentional, classroom inquiries

Readers and Writers Groups
Formed to discuss literary works
or pieces of writing

Professional Book Discussion Groups
Initiated by a common interest to read a
professional book or set of articles

Types of Study Groups and Focus of Discussion.

have been *issues discussion groups*. The discussions are focused around our questions and concerns related to an agreed-upon issue. When appropriate, we choose to read professional articles or to try out engagements in our classrooms.

Other groups are *professional book discussion groups*. The principal study group found it more productive to choose a professional book in the first meeting and then read and discuss that book as a way to focus discussion. Otherwise, the group became mired in everyday problems instead of talking about broader issues. Some teacher study groups have found that centering discussion around a book or set of articles is a good beginning point for a new group. A book can also be helpful if the group is looking at a new topic that is unfamiliar to them.

Study groups can also take the form of a *teacher research group* where members collect data in their settings and bring that research to the group. Sometimes the research is collaborative. In other cases, each member is engaged in a different research focus, and the group serves as a place to share, get support, and receive suggestions from other teacher researchers.

Another focus is that of a *readers group*. The Warren study group decided to read adult novels with a multicultural context. The group meetings consisted of adult literature discussions on these novels. After several sessions of talking about our novels, we reflected on what we had learned about literature discussion and multicultural issues through actually participating in these discussions. Several of us were part of a *writers group*, where we brought our writing for sharing and response during study group sessions. These groups combine active participation in the process with occasional reflection on the implications of their experiences for classroom practice.

As you think about forming a study group in your own area, consider these different formats and types to see which one might meet your needs. Also remember that groups evolve over time. Many of our groups have changed their format over the years. The Warren group started as an issues discussion group and at certain points became a readers group and a professional book discussion group. Some of these changes are the natural result of a group's questions and interests changing over time, and some will come about as a group tries different formats to find the one that works for it.

Start your group at a point that makes sense given your context and questions and, after several months, reflect on what is and isn't working—and make changes. Whenever we stopped to reflect on what was happening in the group, we made changes that resulted in more productive and thoughtful group discussions.

We also found that in order to answer our question of "What is a study group?" we had to look at more than the type of group. Our understandings about study groups grew when we examined what members saw as significant about the study group experience for them both personally and professionally.

What Does a Study Group Add to the Life of an Educator?

Kathy interviewed the members in the two school-based study groups about their perspectives on the value of study groups at the end of our first three years. She asked them to address the following questions (1) Why were they part of the group? (2) In what ways was the group important to them as educators? (3) What wasn't working well for them? She also talked to teachers who had stopped coming to the group. We met each summer to analyze the interviews and to look for patterns in their responses, which we used to form categories around the question, "What was significant about the study group experience?" (Short, Crawford, Kahn, Kaser, Klassen, & Sherman, 1992). The comments in these interviews provide a powerful rationale for why other educators might consider starting a study group in their own contexts.

Building Community and Relationships

At the end of the first year of the study group, the majority of comments related to the opportunity to get to know other teachers in the building. While teachers had taught alongside each other, they did not know each other's thoughts about teaching and did not have a sense of personal or professional community. Teachers felt alone, with little time to get to know others.

> We are like islands. Through the study group, we realize we are not the only ones who have problems or who are making discoveries, and we get to see other people's growth.

> We rarely get to develop collegial relationships. We need to learn to dialogue with others on professional issues. I'm not used to having the chance to discuss practice in a non-evaluative way.

One important role of the study group was to integrate new teachers, student teachers, and specialists into the professional community of the school.

> As a new teacher, I got to know teachers faster because of the group. I was more willing then to talk and open up. I wasn't threatened by them. The group accelerated my becoming part of the faculty.

> I'm a new teacher and I felt lost but the study group made me feel
> that I wasn't alone. Because other people in the group with more
> teaching experience talked about having problems, I realized I
> wasn't alone in my problems.

The study group provided a way to bring together teachers of different
grade levels who were teaching in other hallways and teachers who had
had a history of negative relationships.

> The study group has brought intermediate and primary teachers
> together. We were preparing kids for the next year's teacher but
> we did not have continuity across the whole school.

> Some teachers who didn't relate before at our school, now work
> together. There's more respect for other teachers. We can get be-
> yond our past histories with particular teachers and establish a
> different kind of relationship.

Through the study group, a sense of collegiality and collaboration began to build that included a valuing of self and of other educators in the
school.

> I have a tendency to go to an authority. It's hard for me to feel I
> can gain from someone who is at the same level as I am. It was new
> for me to try and learn by sharing with the group.

> The group has given me a chance to see into people's thinking. I
> might not agree with opinions or approaches but I have gained
> added respect for everyone in some way.

> The meetings every other week to talk and share give security and
> let us see what we have in common. We know what each person
> has to offer. It's nice to know that and to learn about people. It's
> opened up more resources for all of us.

The study group opened up communication between teachers who had
not previously talked, but it also opened up conflict as teachers found
they disagreed with each other. Much of this conflict was already present,
but had not been openly discussed. While conflict increased, so did teachers' willingness to really listen to each other and to share ideas and questions.

> I've sensed an easing on relationships because of the chance to
> discuss and talk. People aren't as afraid. People who haven't ex-
> changed ideas are doing that now. Sometimes, though, it has
> brought more conflict because it brought disagreements out in
> the open.

> There is a different respect level. The personal issues are still a
> problem but there is more of a willingness to listen and allow for
> growth.

We are to the point of listening and asking questions. We are feeling okay to go and ask someone else. That is a positive change in this school. We are getting away from worrying about competition or copying.

Many teachers were relieved to find that others faced problems in their teaching and that they were not alone in dealing with the difficulties that are inherent in schools and classrooms.

People could see that after teaching so many years, I was trying new things in my classroom and maybe that helped them think that they could try, too. I was honest about the problems I faced and that's hard for me to admit.

I liked the discussions about classroom specifics. I realized that other people were concerned and had problems too. It wasn't just me. I felt like I was taken out of isolation. Others are experiencing what I am and some had solutions I could use.

The study group also influenced the relationships and talk among educators outside of the study group and among teachers and students. Even the talk in faculty lounges shifted from complaining to thinking together.

The group created a need for talk with other teachers. It created agendas for talking to each other at lunch, in hallways, and on the drive to and from school. The study group helped me to see who I could talk to about particular issues.

If teachers are sharing and asking for help and feeling comfortable, then that spills over into the classroom. It helps everyone, including our students. They need to feel that there is some sense of family and unity in the school.

Some people didn't offer to share with others before we started this group. Now that we do this as a study group, we spread ourselves out more and talk to more people on the whole faculty.

Because the principal was usually part of the study group, teachers found their understanding of the principal changing and, in turn, principals shifted their views of teachers.

Teacher: Now the principal sees me more as an equal. She feels comfortable supporting what I do and I support her. It's a fun feeling and a change in this school.

Teacher: I thought it was amazing at the last study group when the teachers did not back down from the principal's comment. They felt their own power. They were equal in the group. They felt that their opinion mattered. Their opinions can be different and not wrong.

Principal: I've realized that teachers really are thoroughly thinking through what they are doing in the classroom much more than I had previously thought. Just because a lesson does not go well, doesn't mean the teacher hasn't thought a lot about it.

Principal: By observing teachers in their classrooms and interacting with them in the group, I have gained greater respect for them. I can see examples of situations where in the past I would have said, "I wish this was different" about something I saw in someone's classroom without understanding the *why* behind what was going on. I see that a beginning attempt to make a change could be seen as chaos or disinterest. Now I see what is being attempted and try to make suggestions because of the study group discussions.

Making Connections across Theory and Practice

Members of the groups also commented on the ways in which their dialogue with others helped them think through connections between their beliefs and their practices. Some had well-developed beliefs but weren't sure how to put these beliefs into practice. Others had spent little time reflecting on their beliefs and why they engaged in particular practices in their classrooms. The study group gave them time to think about these connections for themselves instead of jumping on the bandwagon of new fads or district mandates.

In the past, we did it because we were told to, not because we believed in it or really understood how to put it into practice. Now there's more understanding and openness.

I already had beliefs such as that learners can be responsible and constructive learners. What I needed was practice, how to do it in order to move away from teacher centered to collaborative relationships and from abstraction to practice.

Through the study group, I learned the importance of thinking about my beliefs. I was challenged to think about *why* I do things in particular ways. That has carried over to my classroom. I've been putting a lot of focus on *why*— always explaining why we are doing what we are doing. I do this in notes to parents. I show kids district requirements, my plan book, the minute requirements so they know what's going on and why. Students don't automatically love school. They need to know why we do what we do. I share university papers and quotes from them in those papers. I read it to them before I hand it in.

Supporting Curriculum Reform

Many teachers were frustrated with constant demands for curriculum change within the district. They were open to change but resented being forced to make changes on the district's time schedule. They wanted time to focus on one or two areas at a time instead of trying to do a little of everything in their classrooms. The study group provided a powerful alternative that they felt recognized their professionalism and supported them in making significant curricular changes. They noted that change takes time and needs to happen gradually.

> When you see new ideas and there's too much at once, it seems overwhelming. I decided to take one new thing a year and not just dive into everything. When someone tries to do everything, it is threatening.

> I need time to find out about the curriculum at my grade level and have time to think about my teaching. We always have so many new projects from the district all in the same year.

> We need support to make major change. The changes need to be gradual and over time. We were just thrown into the water and told to survive.

> Even if we aren't all doing the same things, we are talking about it and all of us realize that there is more to learn, no matter where we started at.

Teachers came to view the study group as a "zone of safety" within which they could take chances and make mistakes as they explored new curricular ideas.

> The study group has meant support. A place where I feel comfortable, even when the principal's there, in saying how I am feeling about what I am doing. I can ask questions and not be put down. I need support in order to change my teaching.

> The study group makes it less threatening. It's a safe way to get ideas without feeling judged. You can try something new and see what others are doing. You can see that others have problems too.

> I learned that if you believe in something, you keep on going even if it doesn't work out right away. I don't feel like I have to have all the answers any more. It doesn't matter what it looks like in the beginning, you stay with it. You don't quit just because it isn't perfect right away.

> Teachers are so isolated and when you try something new, it goes downhill at first. It's all changing and you don't know if you can count on anything. Unless there's some kind of peer support, very little change actually occurs no matter how many workshops there are.

The voluntary and exploratory nature of study groups was in sharp contrast to the district mandates teachers so often received.

The study group is voluntary so we are not forced. We are told to do so many things by the district. When we can choose to do something, then we are there because we want to. It's nice not to be told to do something. We are encouraged but not told.

The district is sending a message that there is one right way. They are saying *you will*, instead of consider it, take a look, and try it. It would be nice to not be told to do something, but to be encouraged. In the study group, we are able to explore ideas, instead of feeling forced to implement someone else's program.

Teachers need a voice. Our opinion doesn't count for anything and we are not treated as if we are professional people who have some experience with the situation. Study groups give us a place to have a voice.

We need support in developing ideas. We did get materials that gave us support but *people* change people. You can't just buy a program.

Developing a Sense of Professionalism

Teachers saw the study group as an important part of their role as professionals. They didn't come to the group because they felt they needed to make changes in their teaching, but as part of their professional lives as learners.

One way in which the study group supported teachers professionally was that it allowed them to live the process as learners that they wanted to create for their students. For many, the study group was their first experience learning collaboratively with other educators. If they wanted to create collaborative environments with their students, they needed to experience it themselves first.

Children want to learn and create their own learning. It's true for me. I say it and hear it confirmed by others in the group that what's good for adults is good for kids. Through the study group, I experienced the same process of collaboration that I want for my students.

I liked it when we made the agenda, not someone else. We sat back and took time to figure out the agenda.

The study group provided time to learn through dialogue and reflection.

The study group has meant two major things to me— professional support and professional sharing. The professional sharing is more than lounge sharing. In lounge sharing, we may talk about teaching some but it's not the focus of conversation. In study group, we have scheduled topics. I like knowing ahead so I can think about it. I like being with teachers and there's no time to do that. It's a professional support because I hear others talk about their problems and I realize that it's OK not to be perfect. We share what's good and what's not.

I enjoyed getting together on a professional level. The tone wasn't social but was based on what is in the classroom. I want to learn from other teachers. I haven't learned yet to step back and really "see" and learn from my kids. I am getting more of my learning from teachers. I like the interaction, throwing ideas out and getting input.

I have an increased desire to be more specific in my thinking. I am more of a feeling, than a clear thinking, person. I tend to burst out with enthusiasm and get no response because I am not presenting it well. I need to think about how to present what I am thinking so that others will hear me. I am trying to think through issues and questions and be able to more clearly communicate my thoughts to others through the talk in the group.

I always find the group a place to share and get reactions from peers on whether something is valuable and worth pursuing. I get more than one viewpoint on a method and different ways of attacking it. The best thing is sharing ideas.

The study group provided a structure that encouraged teachers to take responsibility for, and remain committed to, their own growth as professionals. Otherwise, they found it too easy to become so busy they had no time for professional learning and so lost sight of what they were trying to think through. They also had no time to celebrate what others were learning and exploring.

Being in the group took the pressure off having to figure it out by myself . . . . The study group added structure for moving away and helped me keep going when the tendency was to quit. Usually when I get bogged down, there's no way to generate ideas to move on. It helped that this kind of support was available and so I continued to try.

I used the group as confirmation, to think harder. I felt accountable for what was going on. I had the responsibility to work on something. Having a formal place to get together to discuss makes me think harder.

Last year I had so much energy because it was all new. This year, the newness wears off, and you might give it up but the study group keeps you moving. This year different people began to try things and experience things. They had the ah-ha's and energy and were asking questions and struggling.

> The group helps me keep up with new research and not stagnate.
> It was a chance for me to feel we are more of a family. I enjoyed the
> time and made the time to go to it. It wasn't a burden. I enjoy
> talking to others and learning from them.

Most important, the study group facilitated a sense of professionalism
and encouraged teachers to feel empowered about their roles within
children's lives and in the school.

> The way to be more powerful and change the present system is to
> be a meeting of professionals who want to talk and think together,
> to try things and come back and talk together.

Conclusion

The answer to our question of "What is a study group?" turned out to be
quite complex. For us, it is a voluntary group of people who come together to talk and create theoretical and practical understandings with
each other. This talk integrates theory and practice, sharing and dialogue
in powerful ways. It is not an inservice or staff meeting but it supports
these other professional meetings. It is a place where educators push their
thinking and support others, but it is not a place where change is imposed on its members or where certain members decide on the needs of
other members. While the groups may be school-based, job-alike, or topic-
centered and function as a discussion group, teacher research group,
readers group, or writers group, all groups share the focus on transforming teaching through dialogue and reflection and on creating a sense of
community among teachers. The power of the study group is based in
actually living a collaborative learning process with each other, not just
talking about that process.

3 How Are Study Groups Organized?

Now come the practical details. How do you actually get a study group up and running? This chapter includes the invitations we offered to initiate a new group and the organizational decisions we made regarding focus and logistics, such as time and place, meeting structure, group size, and roles within the group. The strategies we developed are not a lock-step recipe, but are flexible decisions that grew out of our experiences. These decisions should naturally evolve during the process of building trust and community which supports the dialogue in study groups.

How Do You Get Started?

Starting a teacher study group requires thoughtful decisions and actions that signal a broad, open invitation to other teachers. It's important to immediately send the message that study groups are inclusive communities, not exclusive cliques.

Identifying a Topic

The first step in forming a study group is to identify a topic that is relevant to the specific needs or interests of a majority of staff members. It must invite dialogue and provide substantial opportunities for inquiry in that school context. For example, a number of study groups in Tucson have recently formed around inquiry approaches to curriculum. Many teachers have heard about "inquiry" through articles and conferences and want to explore it with other educators.

Sometimes groups form around a need to investigate divisive issues among educators. At Robins, teachers shared a concern about the role of spelling within the language arts processes. Some felt that lists and tests were still the best approach and others believed that spelling was learned through the writing process and editing. While teachers differed in their theoretical beliefs, all shared a concern about spelling and its role in the classroom.

At other times, the issue may be related to a district mandate or policies, such as occurred when the Tucson schools moved to a literature-based approach to reading. Teachers at Warren and Maldonado were already interested in bringing more literature into their programs, so choosing this topic addressed both teacher interests and district initiatives. Likewise, the Fort Lowell study group focused its attention on thematic instruction when their site decided to pilot a new program on integrated curriculum.

A topic should be specific enough to focus discussion and drive inquiry; it should also be broad enough to lend itself to multiple perspectives related to teaching and learning. It should hold the possibility of being approached from a variety of theoretical or philosophical beliefs. If teachers feel that they must already "belong" to a particular theoretical orientation in order to join the group, many will resist membership.

But this is not to say that a group should be atheoretical. When our study group began discussing the topic of literature-based curriculum, teachers with very different belief systems about the reading process came together to talk about their beliefs and the use of literature in the classroom. Many made shifts toward more collaborative learning approaches, but there were teachers who continued to hold strong transmission views of the reading process. We learned to agree to disagree about particular issues and still continue our conversations.

The most successful study groups are usually ones to which teachers bring many experiences and questions. When the Tucson school district moved to a manipulative-based math curriculum, both the Warren and Maldonado study groups chose to focus their discussions and inquiry on this new approach to teaching math. Besides the fact that this topic was chosen more out of a sense of duty than of genuine interest, most teachers had not had enough practical experience with the new program to form specific questions or identify relevant issues. In contrast to the previous and very successful study group inquiry into literature-based reading approaches, the math discussions yielded little in the way of new insights and became bogged down at the level of sharing activities. The focus on literature worked well because teachers were already trying out engagements with literature in their classrooms and so had many experiences, questions, and issues to bring to the group. We realized later it would have been more productive to have begun by reading and discussing a professional book on mathematical processes and instruction or by requesting several inservice presentations. These experiences would have allowed us to create shared understandings to support further inquiry and dialogue.

The initial decision of the topic may be made in several ways. Continuing groups usually determine their focus at the first meeting of the year. When the Maldonado group met at the beginning of their second year, they brainstormed a wide range of possible topics:

**Brainstorming of Possible Topics
(Maldonado)**

Kidwatching
Journal writing in math
Structure for the math curriculum
Evaluation
Literature groups
Portfolios
Grade books/checklists/field notes/record keeping
Computers in the curriculum
New formats for lesson plans
Supporting new teachers

After discussing these options, the group decided to begin with their shared concern about evaluation and the use of portfolios and later in the year move to a focus on mathematics.

When groups are forming for the first time in a school, the individuals interested in starting a group often decide on the topic in order to offer an invitation to others in the school. The proposed focus should be broad and should offer multiple perspectives so that the group members can define what that focus means to them and the issues and questions they want to discuss. When the Maldonado group selected the broad focus of writing, the issues they discussed within specific meetings included the writing process, characteristics of writers of different age levels, organizational structures for writers' workshops, teacher and peer conferenc-ing, teacher evaluation, and self-evaluation.

Some examples of broad topics we have used which invite multiple perspectives are:

- writing across the curriculum
- integrated thematic teaching/inquiry approaches
- literature-based curriculum
- authentic assessment and portfolios
- creating community
- multicultural issues
- reading instruction

Offering an Open Invitation to the School Staff

It is important that an open, well-publicized invitation to join the study group be made to the entire staff of a school. Typically, the group is begun by a small group of teachers who see a specific need for a study group and make some initial plans to get the group going. At Warren and Maldonado, we made our initial announcement at a staff meeting and followed up with reminder notes in mailboxes and signs posted in the teachers' lounge and workroom. On the day of the meeting, another invitation was extended to all staff members over the intercom. At issue is that *everyone is invited and feels welcome.* People choose for themselves whether or not the study group is for them.

We also made sure that more than one person was involved in making announcements. We wanted to immediately send the message that the study group was not the work of one person, but of a community of learners attempting to gain understanding of issues important to all. Warren had members of the previous study group invite new members to attend the next year's group. When Maldonado decided to begin a separate group at their own school site, faculty who had been in the Warren/Maldonado group shared their experiences with the rest of the staff and invited them to be part of starting a new group of their own.

The Role of the Principal in Initiating Study Groups

The principal can help establish a context that supports the study group and integrates it into the overall structure of the school. In our study groups, both principals had already fostered school environments that invited curricular change. While specific changes were not mandated, they expected teachers to constantly examine their teaching and provided guidance and support through inservices, staff meetings, and individual conferences. This support extended to the study group.

The two principals provided time to introduce the proposal for a study group at a regular staff meeting and indicated their support for the establishment of the group. They worked with teachers to make sure that there was a time and a place for the group to meet and that other school events were not scheduled to conflict with study group meetings. Kathy discovered just how critical this support was when she saw a study group from another school fail primarily because the principal did not put the meetings on the school calendar and other events constantly forced them to reschedule or cancel their meetings.

At Warren and Maldonado, the study group was considered part of the school structure, not a special meeting or course. It went into the yearly calendar much as staff meetings did. Warren teachers were part of various committees that took care of school tasks, and so the principal established a study group committee. This committee handled the logistics of scheduling, meeting with facilitators, and sending out announcements.

Both principals, whether or not they attended meetings, provided explicit support for the group by publicly acknowledging in staff newsletters and meetings that they valued the work and thinking of the group. They provided tacit support through individual conversations about issues discussed in the group and through comments that continually invited teachers to become part of the group. Principals who do not value the study group can unintentionally sabotage a group's success by failing to include it on the school calendar or by failing to acknowledge its value to teachers. We noted that this lack of acknowledgment leads some teachers, especially new teachers, to feel the group is just an "extra" task and not important to their lives as professionals in that school.

Another form of support came through a willingness to provide money for resources requested by the group. Both schools were operating under tight budgets, but when possible, funds were found and made available for copies of articles, professional books, outside facilitators, inservices, and substitutes to allow teachers to observe in other teacher's classrooms.

Ideally we also see the principal as an equal member of the study group who participates in the conversations about teaching. However, the reality that the principal holds a position of power complicates the principal's participation. This issue will be discussed in Chapter 6.

Important as the principal can be to a successful study group, schools in which groups have continued despite a change of principal have been ones where teachers take responsibility for organizing the group. In these situations, the study group has helped to provide cultural and curricular continuity for the staff during changes in administrative personnel.

The First Meetings

The first several meetings of the group are usually spent brainstorming questions and areas of interest, deciding on group norms and logistics, and creating a sense of community among members. We learned quickly that just because we taught together didn't mean that we knew or trusted each other. During our first meeting, Kathy, as the facilitator, had each person answer the question, "If I walked into your house, how would I know that you are a literate person? What would your house tell me about you as a reader and writer?" The sharing brought laughter and a different sense of each person than the educator we knew within the school context. It was an "icebreaker" but it also connected to our focus on literature and curriculum. It signaled that this group was going to be about its members getting to know each other on a personal as well as professional level so that they could break down competitive barriers and share without judgement.

Another initial task is to examine the topic and brainstorm questions and issues the group has about that topic. Usually we use large sheets of chart paper and quickly list as many different issues and questions as group members can identify. We use the following rules of brainstorming:

- all ideas are listed
- ideas are not evaluated or prioritized
- only questions of clarification are allowed

The Warren/Maldonado group brainstormed the following lists of issues about literature-based curriculum:

Brainstorming Chart
Issues/Concerns about Literature-Based Curriculum
(Warren/Maldonado Group)

Kids who fall through the cracks
Integration of literature within the curriculum
How to put together literature sets
Using the literature anthologies
How do you form and manage discussion groups?
Moving kids to longer texts
Role of grammar and spelling
Connecting math and science
Relating math and science to literature
Responses to literature beyond discussion groups
Organizing resources so they are easily accessible
Research findings about literature
Educating parents
Methods for student research
Organization—getting it all to work together
Evaluation
Keeping records
Emergent and struggling readers in literature groups
Balance between student and teacher decision-making   ▶

Meaningful seatwork
Difference between guided reading and literature groups
Use of picture books in the intermediate grades
How do you know when it's working?
What do kids discuss in literature groups?
Conferencing with students

Once ideas are listed, the group examines the lists to see if there are related concerns that can be grouped together. We also prioritize the ones that seem of greatest concern. To make sure that all voices are heard, we sometimes have everyone individually write down their top three concerns from the chart and then each person shares his or her top three to see which ones are shared across group members.

Another example of a process to identify questions is one that Clay used when the Fort Lowell group wanted to explore evaluation of student writing. He asked the group members to meet in small groups to brainstorm and write down their questions about evaluation. These questions were then shared with the whole group to find commonalities and develop a combined list.

Rather than immediately decide on a focus, members were asked to think about this list of questions for the next meeting. At that meeting, the group reviewed and revised their list of questions and then made a decision of where they wanted to start their discussions about evaluation. This process provided the basis for a series of discussions that led teachers to try out new methods of evaluating their students.

We keep the brainstorming charts for later reference. Sometimes the charts are typed as a handout for the group. Other times, the charts are kept on the wall in our meeting space.

A group may also want to brainstorm the norms for group interactions. This type of brainstorming can be especially helpful if members have never been in a study group and are unsure how they operate. At their first meeting, the Fort Lowell group brainstormed the following list of norms:

List of Norms
(Fort Lowell Group)

Take care of yourself
Asking questions is okay

▶

No side conversations
Not too much "homework"
Avoid jargon
Start and end on time
Everyone is important

This list was kept open so members could add to it over time.

Obviously there are major differences in these initial meetings if the study group is meeting for the first time or is a continuing group. Developing a sense of community and discussing the group norms are particularly important if the group is meeting for the first time or has many new members. A continuing group may begin without a particular focus because they know that they will develop a focus together. However, if a group is forming for the first time, having a strong focus that is shared across the school is a key factor for teachers in deciding whether or not to join the group.

We found that sometimes a group goes through an initial "mucking around" phase before they get to their real questions on a particular topic. This is especially true for first-time groups that are used to transmission models of professional development where information is presented to them. The first few meetings of the Warren/Maldonado group were spent discussing schedules and curriculum frameworks before the group talked about literature in the classroom. To some, the first meetings might have seemed "off task" but through our analysis of these meetings, we realized how important these initial discussions were in providing a non-threatening atmosphere for participating in the group and discovering our needs and concerns. For purposes of establishing ownership and commitment, it was important to make sure that everyone felt heard and that they participated in framing the agenda. We needed time to get to know each other and to negotiate a way of interacting and a sense of trust before we could get into more difficult issues of teaching and learning.

Types of Meetings

Most study group meetings will fall into one of the four following categories: (1) brainstorming and selecting a topic; (2) narrowing the topic and identifying questions to explore; (3) dialoguing and exploring issues through the inquiry process; and (4) reflecting on the process and content of the group. We have already described the brainstorming process. Narrowing the topic and identifying questions allows members to focus their attention on issues that have personal relevance for them. It is also the time when the group can think about resources and strategies that will facilitate their inquiry. These sessions occur whenever the group is moving into a new topic. The dialoguing and exploring sessions are the heart of the study group as members examine their questions together. These are the sessions that we describe in most depth throughout this book.

The reflection sessions usually occur when the group feels a need to reassess the direction of the group. We often paused to reflect at the end of the first semester and at the end of the year. In these sessions, we discussed what we had learned, what questions were still unanswered, what new questions had arisen, and whether the topic merited further inquiry. If we decided we were still interested in the topic, and new avenues of exploration were revealed, we continued with that topic. If we felt that the topic was exhausted or no longer held a compelling interest for the group, then we began the cycle anew with a brainstorming session or revisited our original brainstorming chart. We also frequently discussed how we felt the group was functioning and whether we needed to make changes in our structure or in our interactions with each other.

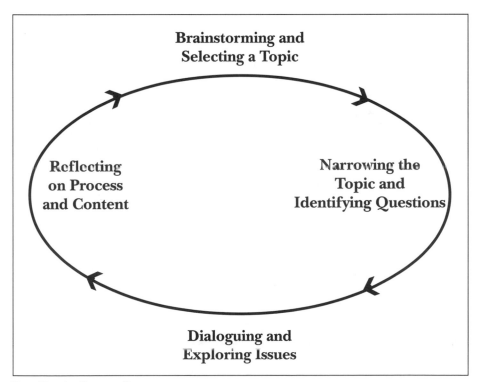

The Study Group Process.

What Logistical Decisions Need to Be Made?

Other important initial decisions relate to the logistics of organizing people, time, facilities, and materials. Some of these decisions are made immediately and others emerge through the work of the group.

In examining our question of "What makes a productive study group session?" we looked at sessions that went well and those that fell apart or were unproductive. This question led us to generate an in-depth picture of group dynamics, facilitation, and structures that support dialogue within the study group. We found that, like our students, we needed a dependable routine and a predictable format to create a safe context in which to learn and grow. These routines and formats were not determined for us but were instead negotiated among the group members. Involving all our voices increased our commitment to the group and allowed us to consider the special needs of our members.

In this section, we share the logistical decisions that have worked for us, but your group will need to keep its own needs in mind as you negotiate what works best for you. The areas we discuss include time, place, resources, group size, roles within the group, and the structure of the meetings.

Time and Place

One of the most important and difficult decisions is finding time to meet within the complicated schedules of educators. There are so many meetings and committees as well as personal commitments that finding a time that suits everyone is extremely difficult. We found that the first step was meeting with the principal to find out the times of other regularly scheduled meetings (staff meetings, child study, after-school programs, university courses). Once we had determined possible times and days, the group established the schedule for the entire semester. Those dates then went into the official school calendar so that meetings did not conflict with other school events.

We found that meeting every other week seemed to work the best for us. Meeting every week would be ideal but was difficult to schedule. Meeting every other week was realistic, given everyone's crowded schedule but was still frequent enough to maintain our momentum as a group. When we met less frequently, we had difficulty continuing our discussions from the previous meeting. However, if a group can only meet once a month, that's better than not meeting at all.

Our process works as follows: We meet after school for an hour-and-a-half on a Tuesday, Wednesday, or Thursday (which day works the best varies by year). Each year we choose one day and stay with that same day the entire year. Changing the day reduces participation because teachers have difficulty remembering when the meeting will be held. At Maldonado, staff meetings were held every other week, so the group decided to have their study group on the same day as the staff meeting, but on the alternating weeks. This worked well because teachers knew they had a meeting every Tuesday.

At Warren, scheduling the staff meeting to alternate with the study group did not work because the principal sometimes needed to have an additional staff meeting or to reschedule the staff meeting to a different week because of holidays or a special event. Either the staff meeting or the study group ended up being canceled. Having the two on different days meant that occasionally teachers had both meetings in the same week, but for the most part they were on alternating weeks.

Because our schools start at 8 o'clock in the morning, meeting immediately after school works the best for us. We begin the study group at 2:15 p.m., five minutes after the children leave the school. This means that occasionally a teacher is late due to an unscheduled parent meeting or other school duties, but for the most part, because the meetings are scheduled ahead of time, teachers come on time. In schools that start at a later time, study groups have met in the morning before school begins. The principal study group has always met early in the morning because principals have such difficulty getting away from school, particularly at the end of the day.

Our study groups meet after school, and so half of our meeting is on school time and half is on teachers' personal time. Because the group is voluntary, this does not create contractual problems but teachers would prefer that the study group be part of their school day. In some schools where children are not bused to school, the schedule is adjusted so that teachers have an early-release day one day a week. The children are in school an extra fifteen minutes a day, four days a week, and leave one hour early one day a week. Study groups meet on the early-release day during school time every other week. The other weeks are used for grade level meetings, staff meetings, and inservices.

Both the time and the place need to be chosen for the greatest convenience of the participants. The meeting should be as easy as possible for participants to attend. At Warren, the study group always met in the school library. This was a central location and could be set up ahead of time so that everything was ready as soon as school was dismissed. At Maldonado, the meetings were held in various classrooms. The students in that classroom arranged the tables before they left. Teachers had an opportunity to see each others' rooms and to ask that particular teacher questions about the room and curriculum. The disadvantage of this arrangement was that the room changed with each meeting. Sometimes teachers wandered the halls looking for the meeting. The facilitator began to post a sign announcing the time and place in the staff lounge on the day of the meeting to cut down on this confusion. Another group met in the lounge but found that there was too much traffic and that teachers who were not members resented the group taking over the lounge.

The principal study group has found that they need to meet in a central location that has easy access in terms of traffic, roads, and parking. Generally we use an elementary school located close to a major street near the center of the city but not downtown, where traffic is difficult. Within the school, we need a room with tables where teachers or students are not going in and out of that room at the beginning of the school day.

Group Size

Decisions about the size of a group has an impact on the nature of the relationships and the amount of talk time available for individual members. Our experience is that ten to twenty members seems to work best. Since it's inevitable that some members are absent at any one meeting, this size means that seven to fifteen people are usually present on each occasion.

However, a smaller size can provide for more intense discussion. At one point, the Maldonado study group went from fifteen members down to five members who attended on a regular basis. Initially the group felt defeated and saw their smaller size as a sign of failure. As they looked at the productiveness of their sessions, however, they realized that their best discussions had occurred when there were only five present. Their discussions were more focused on their particular needs and those that remained were committed.

On the other hand, the combined Warren/Maldonado group at one time went up to twenty-five to thirty members. Initially, this caused a great deal of concern. While there were some problems with fewer people having an opportunity to talk and the loss of some of the intimacy and closeness we had felt the previous year, we did feel that the group was successful. Because we had already met for a year, we had established a sense of community that supported discussion and sharing so the size did not intimidate most people. We did find that the facilitator had to work harder in being aware of participants who wanted to share but weren't willing to push their way into the conversation and so were getting overlooked. We also more frequently moved into small groups during our discussions.

Size does make a difference in the broader influence of the group. Our experience is that when the study group is limited to a small group of individuals, those individuals benefit but the broader school community does not. The Maldonado teachers started a study group at their school and invited other staff members to join them because they wanted to create a stronger school community. As members of the Warren/Maldonado group, they were individually benefiting from the discussions, but they didn't see the kind of schoolwide change which they observed occurring at Warren.

The central issue is not how large or small the group is, but whether or not group members are able to talk openly and honestly with each other about educational issues. While there are ideal sizes, the reality of life is rarely the ideal so we simply look at our size and figure out a way to make it work for us.

Resources

Another initial logistical decision is whether the group will use particular resources to support their talk. In some cases, these resources are the focus of the group discussion and at other times, they are brought into the group as needed.

Professional readings—a book or articles—can help a group focus on the topic and provide a starting point for discussion. They can also support a group that is exploring a new topic and needs to build shared understandings before they can move into in-depth discussions and classroom explorations.

The principal study group found that they needed a professional book to give them a common point for discussion and to introduce the "big" ideas. Otherwise, it was too easy to stay mired in everyday problems. They found that books with short chapters that dealt primarily with larger theoretical ideas and provided a few practical examples worked the best. Books such as *Life in a Crowded Place* (Peterson, 1992) and *Renewing America's Schools* (Glickman, 1993) worked well.

NCTE has created several kits of materials for study groups that include teleconferences, videotapes, articles, journals, and books around particular topics such as literature discussion groups, spelling, and reading instruction. These materials are available individually or as a packaged kit. The study group can determine which of these materials they wish to purchase for their group. In addition, they can join a listserv with other study groups across the country to discuss issues.

Other organizations whose materials have been helpful in providing resources for study groups include the International Reading Association (IRA), the Association of Supervision and Curriculum Development (ASCD), and the National Council of Teachers of Mathematics (NCTM). We have also used many professional books from publishers such as Heinemann and Stenhouse.

Other resources that some study groups have used are the national standards that various subject-area groups have been developing over the last several years. The study group provides a format where groups can examine national standards such as *Standards for the English Language Arts* (published in 1996 by NCTE and IRA) and use these as a basis for developing their own set of standards. *The Literate Life: Exploring Language Arts Standards within a Cycle of Learning* (NCTE, 1997) is a booklet that supports study groups in dialoguing about what they value in the teaching and learning of language arts in their school context.

While these books and resources can provide a valuable support to a study group, they can also get in the way of groups exploring their own issues and questions. Members tend to discuss the issues raised by the book rather than their own issues. Depending on the group's focus and the particular group members, it may be more productive to focus the discussion around the questions and concerns of group members rather than a particular book. An article or book may still be used occasionally to think about a specific issue but these readings are suggested *after* the group has made a decision on a particular focus.

Additional Components to the Study Group

Some groups have added components to the study group that go beyond the actual meetings. These components include receiving district increment credit for participating in the study group and adding observation and consultation in classrooms.

The Tucson school district offers salary increment credits each year through a range of district inservices. Because we believed that the study group was a valuable form of professional development that should be available for increment credit, Clay pursued this possibility. While there was some concern that teachers would receive district credit "just for talking," Clay used his previous experiences to talk with district administrators about the focus, activities, and benefits of teacher study groups. In order to receive district credit, Clay added a mid-year and end-of-the year evaluation/reflection, but otherwise the group functioned as a regular study group. The district credit gave the teachers recognition for their commitment to professional growth and was an additional incentive for them to stay actively involved.

Several group members who were involved in graduate programs were able to negotiate independent study credits toward their degrees for their participation in the group. They kept a journal of their responses to individual meetings and then wrote a reflection on the experience for their university advisor.

During the first two years of the study group, Kathy was available one day a week to work in classrooms. A sign-up sheet with open time slots was posted in the staff workroom and anyone who wanted to work with her signed up. On these occasions, Kathy interacted with students in small groups or as individuals, team taught alongside the teacher, taught demonstration lessons, observed teachers and students to provide another perspective on classroom life, or conferenced with teachers about the issues that were of primary concern to them. Teachers made differing decisions about whether to have Kathy participate in their classrooms. Several teachers signed up each week, others signed up on an occasional basis, and still others never signed up. The agenda for Kathy's work in the classroom was initiated and determined by the teacher, although she and the teacher did negotiate the specifics of how they might work at that agenda.

This option was very important to some of the teachers in the group who were making major shifts in their thinking about curriculum. Although the study group was a place to share theory and practice, the classroom visits enabled teachers to go into greater depth with their thinking or to explore other paths than the study group agenda. For example, several teachers used the classroom visits to work on particular strategies over time in a way that made sense to them. Sandy explored inquiry studies using broad concepts. Kathy's visits enabled Sandy to see the possibilities for using literature effectively within this study by providing suggestions and responses on a weekly basis. This kind of support coupled with the study group discussions gave Sandy a foundation in literature-based curriculum that made a lifelong change in her teaching. Other teachers used the support of the classroom visits to work on writing or on portfolios. The classroom support gave study group members a way to talk with each other about their experiences in more concrete ways in the group.

Classroom visits by different professionals are another option that could be offered in your school. For example, you could make arrangements for a visit by a curriculum specialist, a resource teacher, your principal, the librarian, the school psychologist, district resource personnel, or a local teacher educator. Such visits are not essential to a study group, but they do add a significant dimension. However, it is important that the visitor become a member of the study group and be available to come into classrooms on a regular basis. Because these visits take the form of a collaborative relationship, they need to be initiated by the teacher and not mandated. The person must be willing to think with teachers, offer new perspectives, and challenge assumptions, not judge.

Through the study group discussions, teachers realized that they wanted to know more about each other's classrooms and have time to observe what was happening. Both schools added a "Teacher-to-Teacher" staff-development option where teachers could visit other teachers at their school or in another school. A substitute teacher was hired for the school one day a week and each week, one person was released from the classroom for a day.

At Maldonado, teachers who were interested in this option turned in a plan to the principal in which they noted whom they wanted to observe and the professional literature they wanted to read in their area of interest. This option was funded through special state funds available for professional development.

The teachers then spent a half-day visiting in classrooms and the rest of the day reading professional materials based on their special interest. They were then asked to write a reflection on the experience to give to the principal. Thus, one teacher who was interested in literature discussion visited a teacher who used literature circles on a regular basis. She made arrangements ahead of time with that teacher and chose several articles and chapters to read. In another instance, two teachers who were interested in team teaching visited a school where classes were being team taught.

At Warren, each teacher was released for one day each semester to visit in other classrooms. This occurred during the third year of the study group when teachers had become comfortable with one another and were interested in the diverse methods of teaching in the school. Some observed classrooms when particular events were occurring, such as a literature study or shared reading. In one case, an intermediate teacher observed primary classrooms to see a "big book" lesson. She was surprised to find out it was actually a reading lesson done with, literally, a big book. These observations were another way to cut down on isolation and encourage sharing among teachers.

Structure of the Meetings

Another logistical issue is deciding on a general structure for the meeting—a routine that group members can depend on and easily follow. Our routine was to begin with sharing, move into a focused discussion, and then end with decisions on our focus for the following meeting.

Most of our study group meetings are an hour-and-a-half in length. We usually spend the first twenty minutes in sharing and getting started with the meeting. Once we move into our focus, it often takes thirty minutes or so before we get deeply into our focus for the day and find the issues we want to discuss. We need at least ten minutes at the end to talk about what we want to discuss at our next meeting and what we will do to prepare for that meeting. Ideally, a two-hour meeting would be the best length because we often find that we are deep in discussion when it is time to end. However, many teachers have personal commitments that do not allow them to stay beyond 3:30 p.m. so we need to end on time or they are excluded from our decision making. Often a few will continue their conversations after the meeting officially ends. This structure of sharing, discussions, and decisions has worked well for us. It's a flexible structure that meets our diverse needs as a group.

Beginning with sharing has served a variety of purposes. On a practical level, it has been a way to deal with stragglers—people who are always late as well as those who get caught in the hallway by a parent or child. Initially, we waited to begin until everyone was there but found we were losing valuable time and some were coming later and later because they knew we wouldn't start on time. We decided to begin sharing with whoever was present at our starting time. Those who arrive late aren't interrupting a focused discussion because the sharing is a more informal conversation that they can easily join. The sharing provides a transition from the intensity of working with children to the study group discussion. Members make the mental shift and gradually relax as they share informally with each other.

In addition, sharing creates a sense of community as members learn more about each other. They gradually build the sense of trust and respect that is essential to be willing to engage in difficult discussions about teaching. During the sharing time, members can talk about any issue, not just the ones that are the group's focus. Teachers share their excitement about an event in their classroom or lives, show a student's artifact, talk about a problem or concern, pass on information, or tell about a new professional resource or children's book. Sometimes, the sharing is a time for venting frustration over a new district or school policy. Through this sharing, we find that we have the opportunity to hear ideas from many more members, get to know others personally, find out what teachers are doing in their classrooms, show our support and valuing of each other, and see how others are growing professionally.

Sometimes teachers shared their excitement at new curricular engagements as Pat did when she started a meeting by saying "I'm dying to share." She had brought the sketches that her first graders had made of the meaning of a book she had read aloud to them. It was the first time she had tried Sketch to Stretch (Short & Harste, 1996) and she was excited by her students' responses and thinking. Other times, teachers used the group as a sounding board to think through their practice. Maria shared how she was approaching reading in her bilingual classroom. While she was worried that the other teachers would judge her for using the basal, she wanted to talk about what was working for her. "I feel like I need a security blanket. I need something structured to hold on to right now so I do one or two literature books and then I go back to my basal reader." In both cases, others in the group responded with questions and affirmation.

For some teachers, the sharing was the most important part of the study group and the reason they attended. We struggled with the tension of meeting the different needs of group members. Some primarily see the group as a place to share and build community and others see it as a place to push themselves professionally and consider new ideas. Starting with sharing and then moving into the focus meets both needs.

The heart of our meeting is the focused discussion of the issues, experiences, or reading that the group has agreed on for the meeting. This discussion determines whether members feel that the group is or is not productive for them. As you can imagine, there are many issues related to focusing the discussion and these are discussed in Chapter 4.

The final part of the meeting is usually spent reflecting on the discussion and negotiating a topic for the next meeting. Once the group has made a decision on the focus or issues for the next meeting, they also need to decide whether they will read or engage in an experience to prepare for that focus.

The structure we have described here has worked well for us, given our context and meeting time. You may find that a different structure will work better for you. The principal study group, for example, found that when they started their meetings with sharing, they never got to their focus. Their lives were so full of frustrations that the sharing took over the meeting. While they valued this time to talk about their problems, they came to the group to think about bigger theoretical issues. There was no other place where they could discuss these broader issues and pull back from the day-to-day problems in their schools. The group decided to start with announcements, move to the focus, and then take the last twenty to thirty minutes to share.

Meeting in Small Groups

Another variation in the structure is moving between whole-group and small-group discussions. We used small groups when our group was large, so more individuals would have a chance to talk. We have also used small groups when it is clear that members have different issues they want to discuss, which are related to the session focus. In a Maldonado discussion about mathematics instruction, some group members wanted to talk about organizing the math curriculum around long-range big ideas, while others wanted to discuss specific organizational structures and activities.

In addition, small groups are advantageous when the members have brought specific items to share that would be difficult to see or boring if everyone shared theirs individually. For example, at the beginning of our second year, we met in small groups to share the specifics of how each of us was trying to create a sense of community in our classrooms. When everyone had tried a different kind of portfolio, we shared the specifics of what each person had done in small groups before moving to a large-group discussion. During our discussion of field notes, everyone brought field notes from their classroom to our meeting, so we began by sharing these in small groups. Teachers could actually look at each others' notes. We then came back to our large-group session and listed the issues we wanted to discuss further about field notes.

We also found it necessary to move to small groups when we were meeting as a readers or writers group. The Warren group decided to engage in adult literature discussions and so read novels that were first discussed in small groups before returning to whole-group sharing. When a number of us met with other colleagues in a writers group, we broke into groups of three to four to share and respond to our writing.

Group members had differing responses to small groups. Some did not like small groups because they were afraid of missing ideas that someone shared by being in the "wrong" small group. One teacher worried that "all the confident people will sit together. I don't want to sit in one group where everyone is struggling." Still others liked to stay with the whole group because it broadened the spectrum of ideas being considered and created a strong sense of community. However, some viewed the small groups as a way to discuss a topic in depth and have time to ask and respond to questions such as, "Why are you doing it this way?" "What was the purpose of that?" These members put an emphasis on dialogue and saw the small groups as a structure in which there was more opportunity for people to talk and to focus discussion among a smaller group of colleagues.

In meetings where we use small groups, we usually begin the meeting as a whole group for our sharing. Once we define our focus for the meeting, we meet in small groups. Sometimes the small groups are formed by whoever happens to be sitting together; and other times the groups meet by age level, interests, or some other relevant criteria. We come back to a large group and take about twenty minutes for each small group to share highlights from their discussion and to raise issues that the group might want to consider as a whole.

What Kinds of Roles Are Needed within the Study Group?

When we first began our study group, there were no distinct roles that members assumed beyond that of facilitator. We have devoted a separate chapter to discussing the complexity of this role. When we analyzed what was happening in group meetings, we also identified several other roles important to the smooth functioning of the study group. These roles are those of the notetaker and the timekeeper.

Notetaker

Initially, Kathy took field notes of our meetings and then used these to write a one-page summary that was distributed in teachers' boxes a week before the next study group meeting. We saw the notes as playing a research function and so when Kathy stopped serving as facilitator and notetaker, the notes dropped out of both groups midway through the third year. They didn't seem to have a "real" role within the group process. However, when we analyzed data from the groups the following summer, we found that both study groups had experienced problems that were related to the absence of the field notes. In the Maldonado group, members lost valuable time at the beginning of their meetings trying to reconstruct their previous meeting and to remember what they had decided as the focus for that meeting. Sometimes, they simply kept on sharing for the entire meeting because they didn't have a sense of focus. They also had difficulty remembering when and where the meetings were going to be held, especially members who had missed the previous meeting.

These problems led both groups to add the role of notetaker to their meetings the following year. At the end of each meeting, someone volunteered to be the notetaker for the following meeting. This person did not try to write down everything that was said during the meeting but kept a list of the key issues, topics, and questions that were discussed and the decisions made at the end of the meeting. This list of key issues could then be read back to the group at the end of their meeting as a summary of what they had discussed and to help them select discussion topics for the next meeting. Other group members could add to the list if they felt that the notetaker had left out key ideas. The notetaker also kept track of issues or ideas that the group wanted to come back to in a later session.

During the meeting, issues or questions often came up that had not been discussed at that particular time for various reasons. The notetaker wrote down these issues and questions so the group could decide whether they wanted to address them in future meetings.

A summary of these notes was then typed up (no more than one page) and sent out to everyone in the faculty. Sometimes the summary was written as a paragraph and other times as a list. The notes always included the time, place, and focus of the next meeting. By sending the notes to everyone in the school, and not just the current group members, other faculty felt informed and invited to the group. Thus, if the group was moving into a new topic that interested them, they could join the group.

The following examples of notes show two different styles of notetaking that emerged from our groups, one rather comprehensive and the other very brief.

 **Maldonado Study Group Notes
September 22**

Sharing

- Irma shared bilingual books from her classroom. Her sharing led us to discuss Spanish literature for children.
- Clay wants to have his students observe in other classes. He will train them how to observe before they come to your room. If you would like to participate, see him.
- Sonya and Maria shared their experiences at the math conference. Everyone felt a strong need for more information regarding what the district is doing with math.

▶

■ Sharon went to a Columbus Inservice from the Fine Arts department. She has some great handouts she's willing to share with anyone who is interested.

Topic for this Session: Year-Long Plans

We talked about the district requirement that we turn in year-long plans and created different models for these plans that fit a collaborative approach to curriculum. We met in small groups to share drafts of our initial attempts at different formats. Many were uncomfortable with determining ahead of time exactly what topics will be studied for the entire year. We wanted to develop plans that reflected our thinking about the possibilities for how the curriculum might develop, realizing that it would change as we worked with students. Gloria and Kathleen shared how they use a broad concept like Harmony or Change to brainstorm possible directions and put those into a large web. They then gather and list resources such as books and activities. They incorporate the district curriculum into this brainstorming before the start of school and then add the children's ideas once school begins. They also put in their weekly schedule which lists the daily blocks of time and the kinds of things kids are doing during those times. This "planning to plan" gives them direction and flexibility.

Topic for Next Session: Math

We decided to spend the semester looking at math instruction. To get us started, everyone agreed to bring what they are currently working on with students to our next meeting.

> **Facilitator for next meeting:** Clay
> **Notetaker for next meeting:** Gloria
> **Treats:** 2nd and 3rd grade teachers
> **Room:** Clay's room, #23

Maldonado Study Group Notes
February 9

Topic: Evaluation of writing within writing process
         Writing portfolios
         Conferences with students
         Length of conference
         Questions to ask
         Taking field notes   ▶

Our next meeting is Tuesday, February 23 at 2:15 in Room 19, Kathleen's classroom.

> Facilitator: Kathleen
> Focus: Evaluating writing through examining children's miscues.
> To do: Read article by Yetta Goodman (on file in faculty room)

Anyone who is interested is invited to join us.

Yet another example of notes comes from the Maldonado study group where members developed a form that the notetaker could quickly fill out and distribute. This form was also placed in a faculty notebook that was kept in the staff lounge (See example, p. 52).

Timekeeper

Another role that is helpful is that of timekeeper. We found that it is difficult for the facilitator to facilitate the conversation and group dynamics, keep track of time, *and* break into a conversation to announce a transition. In fact, the facilitator can be misunderstood and seen as cutting someone off when taking a double role of facilitator and time-keeper.

Several study groups have a timekeeper whose role is to announce when it is time to begin the meeting, when twenty minutes have passed and it is time to move to the focus of the meeting, and when only fifteen minutes are left in the session and the group needs to stop so they can negotiate for the next meeting. The timekeeper's announcements are sometimes ignored because the group is in the middle of important conversations but they are at least aware that there are time constraints.

Conclusion

While the issues that study groups consider are complex and difficult, the structures that support discussions of these issues must be simple and easy to maintain. Given the realities of teachers' lives in schools, there is little time to maintain complex and time-consuming structures. Our decisions were based on what made sense in our specific contexts. There were many additional elements that we could have added but the structures would have been difficult to maintain without a great deal of support such as someone having release time in the building.

First and foremost, the structures we developed had to support our major goal of engaging in professional dialogue about issues significant

NOTES _Ch. 2 – Posit. Disc_____   DATE _Sept. 10_____

Agenda Topic: _____Keep It Cheap (what does this mean?_)

Facilitator: _____Sharon_____
Notetaker: _____Ruth_____
Timekeeper: _____Danielle_____

Responses:
- if prob. doesn't "self-eliminate" → not working   *manag. tech*
- Pay me now or pay me later
- all little things piling up = stress
- In good class – ⅓ of class off task all the time !!
- Good discipline protects students
- "we are on our own"/change won't come from top
- Folklore of manag. → not enough to be fair, firm,
  Consistent, follow-through
- Reward for disrupt. its own reward → peers

Daily disruptions in our classes / What are we doing
                                              that works?

- pencils (sharpening, lost, fighting over) — use crayon
                                                broken pencils
- restroom   at table
                                           — Passes, limit per week
- transitions   — time limit/points
- announcements from office
- not listening (playing, side
                           conversations)
- arguing continues in class
        after lunch break — class meetings
- "I can't" – "I don't get it"
- Centers / small groups
- nurse's office

Next Meeting:
Topic: _Read Ch. 3 / Structures, Rules, & Routines_
Facilitator: _____Ruth_____
Notetaker: _____Linda_____
Timekeeper: _____Sharon_____

Form Used by Notetaker.

to our lives as teachers. Anything that interfered or took away from the talk needed to be reconsidered.

It was important that these structures remain flexible and open-ended so that we could make changes as the group's needs and interests changed and so we could remain open to other faculty members joining the group. This was a group for anyone in the school who wanted to think reflectively about teaching, not just those who subscribed to a particular philosophy.

It was also critical to us that the structures facilitated group decision-making and negotiation. The issues we discussed needed to come from the group itself. While this negotiation took time, it was essential to the very nature of the group.

Lastly, we looked for convenience and routine. We wanted to make it as easy as possible to attend the meetings and participate in the discussions. We didn't want to have to negotiate elaborate formats each time we met. We searched for a routine that we could use with small variations so we could get down to the discussions themselves.

The "right" answers for each of the practical questions in this chapter will change in different school contexts. The answers will also change for the same group over time. Only the questions and issues will remain the same.

4 How Are Study Groups Facilitated?

If study groups were a place to disseminate information, then facilitation would not be an issue. However, study groups are complicated by their very nature—people of varied experiences coming together to learn from each other in an environment where there is no agreed-upon "expert" to provide definite answers. A further complication is that educators are often unaccustomed to learning from others who are at similar points in professional growth. In this context, the need for a facilitator becomes apparent.

The facilitator doesn't play the visible, directive role of a presenter in a workshop or inservice. Instead, the facilitator functions behind the scenes facilitating talk and decisions but carefully not making those decisions for the group. The facilitator doesn't dominate the talk but often offers a comment or suggestion at a critical point. For the most part, the role is one of process and not content.

We discovered through our analysis of the transcripts and discussions that the role of an effective facilitator involves the following behaviors:

- developing strategies and language to support others in sharing their expertise
- helping participants establish credibility by supporting their connections between theory and practice
- creating a trusting environment by mediating personal conflicts, taking time to reflect on the group process, openly discussing personal interrelationships, and relating personal issues to a broader context of school and topic
- negotiating individual agendas and developing a shared group agenda
- encouraging and acknowledging the contributions of a variety of voices so that individuals do not dominate the group "talk time"
- keeping the conversation flowing and helping members reflect by asking questions and summarizing comments
- reinforcing and monitoring the structure and focus of discussion, particularly at the beginning and ending of sessions

■ making available resources that enhance the conversation, be it topical or relative to the process of group dialogue

■ stepping back from participating as actively in the discussion as one might like and yet, at the same time, knowing when to share

Most of these behaviors are described in greater depth in this chapter although some of the interpersonal issues of group dynamics are discussed in Chapter 6. This chapter focuses on the facilitator's role throughout the study group meeting and the advantages and disadvantages of the different possibilities for selecting a facilitator.

What Does a Facilitator Do?

The major responsibilities of the facilitator are to enact the structures that the group has established for the meeting and to support productive talk in the group. As facilitators we spent time before the group met to think about the focus for that session and possible directions the group might take. We considered possible experiences, articles, or materials that might support the discussion. We did not assume that any of these ideas would be used, but we tried to be prepared with options to suggest in case the discussion bogged down.

In the Maldonado study group, Susan developed a planning sheet that she used as a facilitator. On this sheet, she jotted down her plans and a range of ideas and questions that she could pose if needed to encourage discussion (See example, p. 56).

Starting the Meeting

We found that the facilitator usually needed to take a more active role at the beginning of the meeting. It was especially important for the facilitator to invite the group members to immediately start sharing at the opening time instead of waiting until everyone is there. Clay, for example, began a meeting by saying, "It's 2:15, so let's get started. Our discussion today will be on classroom management, but first, who has something to share? Anybody have something exciting that's been happening or a concern they want to bring to the group?"

Typically, the sharing begins with a couple of quick announcements. One issue we ran into was when our sharing time was taken over with various announcements about other meetings or events. The group resented their sharing time disappearing in a flurry of announcements and so the facilitator asked members to be more selective in those announcements, using the staff newsletter when possible. People were asked

AGENDA TOPIC: *Posit. Disc. in Class.* DATE: *Sept. 10*
(Fred Jones)

Facilitator: *Sharon*
Notetaker: *Ruth*
Timekeeper: *Danielle*

I.   Sharing (20 mins.)

II. Discussion (60 mins.)
    A. Recap of issues discussed and decisions made at previous meeting. *(Read notes — summarize)*
    B. Focus question or comment: _____
       What were your responses to Chap. 2?
    C. Negotiate format: _____
    D. NOTES:

(Penny) We know probs. — what do we DO about them?!!
— ask Ruth to share about workshop
— Some ans. coming up in Ch. 3

List causes of disrupt. in our classes

What are we doing now that works?
doesn't work?

III. Plan next meeting: (10 mins.)
    (Notetaker reviews notes of meeting's discussion)
    A. Topic: *"Rules & Routines"* *(Prep. read Ch 3 — make note*
    B. Facilitator: *Ruth* *of other disrupts. not*
    C. Notetaker: *Linda* *already on our list. Ideas*
    D. Timekeeper: *Sharon* *for working w/ them.)*

Facilitator Planning Sheet.

to limit an announcement to one minute. In another group, members signed up ahead of time to make announcements.

Usually after fifteen to twenty minutes of sharing, the facilitator checks with the group to see if they are ready to move into the focus or if anyone else wants to share. Leslie, for example, asked, "Is there anyone else who has something to share or are you ready to move into talking about our focus?" This signals that it's time to move on, but doesn't cut off sharing if someone has something important.

As the group moves to the focus, the facilitator summarizes the previous meeting and reminds members of the decisions that were made about the agenda. The facilitator sometimes suggests a possible format for the discussion and asks for the group's response.

In one meeting, Kathy signaled the move to focused discussion by stating, "The last several meetings we have actually been doing literature circles by discussing a shared book and also by having text-set discussions. We decided last time that our focus today was talking about doing literature groups with kids as a follow-up to those experiences." Since the group had not decided on a format for the meeting, she suggested a possible format:

> We started talking about literature circles over a year ago and many of you have worked on these discussions in different ways so I wondered about starting our discussion by having people talk about what has been successful for them. And then we could move from there into the kinds of issues, questions, and problems that you want to think more about. It seems overwhelming to start with problems, especially when things have worked well for many of you. Does that fit with what you thought we would do today? Does anyone have a different suggestion for how we might proceed?

Changing the Agenda

For a study group to be responsive to the changing needs of members, there are times when sharing leads to a spur-of-the-moment change in agenda. Often this occurs when a pressing need develops through the course of a school day and spills over into the group. At various times, members have voiced concerns about issues, such as student discipline, district mandates, or personal feelings of anger, despair, or frustration about particular students or events. Sometimes talking about the issue during sharing is enough, but at other times there is a larger issue beneath the specific concern or frustration that is productive for the group to discuss. When the sharing appears to be taking over the meeting, the facilitator should always remind the group of their previously agreed-upon agenda, but then let the group decide whether to continue with the emerging issue or return to their previous topic.

At one particular meeting, the teachers at Warren were extremely upset over a new district policy on assessment that was going to take a great deal of time with little benefit to children or teachers. We decided to delay our discussion of our focus and talk about the new policy instead. After spending some time venting our frustrations, we talked about possible short-term and long-term responses to the new policy. The short-term responses focused on ways to deal with the new assessment in the classroom and the long-term responses on ways to get the policy changed.

Sometimes a teacher raises an individual problem of great concern to them personally during the sharing. The group has to make a decision of whether to drop the group agenda to support that teacher in brainstorming and thinking through the issue. We found that there wasn't one answer to this issue. Sometimes, we did drop the group agenda because it was clear that the teacher was in crisis and needed support or because that person had not previously shared and was opening up for the first time. Other times, the discussion moved to larger issues that everyone in the group shared and wanted to discuss.

One September, a fourth-grade teacher in the Warren group shared that his students were "very low in their reading and just don't seem to be focusing in." His statement put everyone on the edge of their seats, especially the third-grade teachers. Initially, the group focused specifically on the validity of the tests he had given to students, but then larger issues started emerging. At that point, Kathy commented to the group, "We are past the time when we usually move to our focus. Do you want to continue discussing reading levels or move to our focus on multicultural issues?" The group only briefly glanced her way before intently continuing their discussion that went on to issues such as the differences between students who moved into the school and those who were there throughout their elementary years, why a particular class of students sometimes experiences problems at every grade level no matter what teachers do, and the difference between expecting that students be on grade level at the end of the year and expecting students to experience a year's growth. The group moved from blaming previous teachers to a very productive discussion about the kinds of teacher research they needed to do to understand and support a large group of students who all seemed to be experiencing major learning problems.

On the other hand, there were particular teachers who always had personal needs and questions. If we addressed these needs, then other teachers started dropping out of the group because their needs weren't being met. Some of the strategies we used as facilitators were to suggest resources or ask if a group member would be willing to meet individually with that teacher to talk about those issues.

We also realized that some teachers who shared frustrations didn't expect us to solve the problem, but needed us to listen with empathy and concern. We tended to jump into a "Let's solve this problem" mode too quickly in our eagerness to help. At the end of January, Kathleen brought a question that was of great concern to her, "What do you do when you've worked hard the whole year to build community and get the kids to a certain point, and then a new child comes in who doesn't fit into your community and rejects everything?" The group felt her frustration and took time to think about possible responses. None of these suggestions seemed to help until Sandy sympathized saying, "One kid can change the whole room and sometimes you try everything and you just have to get to May." Several other teachers also empathized with Kathleen about how hard it was to have a new child change the classroom community. It was immediately clear that their empathy was what she needed at that point in time.

Another issue is for the facilitator to make sure that the individuals involved in a particular incident or problem are part of the discussion. In one meeting, we discussed an upsetting incident involving fifth-grade girls in the school. Members wanted to discuss this issue, not to place blame on anyone, but out of concern. The problem was that the teacher of the girls was unable to be at the meeting and was upset to learn that the incident had been discussed without her. She felt that she could have provided contextual information and benefited from the discussion. The discussion was a thoughtful one, but she felt that her presence would have cleared up many of the issues and allowed the group to focus in a more productive way. She also felt that it was a violation to discuss anyone's students or class when that teacher was not present. Fortunately this study group had a long history together and strong relationships or this incident could have been destructive. In this instance, the facilitator should have suggested delaying discussion until the teacher could be present and encouraged the group to proceed with the previously agreed-upon agenda.

Focusing the Discussion

During the session, the major responsibility of the facilitator relates to monitoring group dynamics and to keeping the discussion focused in a productive manner. The issues of group dynamics will be discussed in Chapter 6. Keeping the conversation focused without dictating the direction of the group's discussion is often a challenge but is essential to the success of the group. The heart of the study group is its ability to engage in dialogue about a focused issue, rather than skipping from topic to topic without enough discussion on any of them for in-depth thinking to occur.

Typically, the discussion begins with the facilitator stating the focus and asking the group to state issues related to the topic that they think are important. This invitation allows group members to define what they see as the topic and the key issues related to that topic. By quickly noting these issues, the group establishes an overview for their discussion and identifies differences in how members are defining or viewing the issue.

We found on numerous occasions that while everyone had agreed on a particular topic for the session, they had completely different perspectives on that topic and what they thought was going to be discussed. Starting out by quickly noting the issues and perspectives set the context for a more productive discussion. To initiate a discussion at Maldonado, Clay commented, "We agreed last time that we were going to talk about our plans for management. Is that what everyone is prepared to do today?" Mary immediately commented, "But we were going to talk about issues of control. And in my opinion I don't see management and control as the same thing." Clay responded by asking, "Could you expand on that a little bit?" This comment led the group into a discussion about control and classroom management that made it clear that teachers had very different definitions and understandings of those terms and so had different conceptions on the meeting focus. Without this initial discussion, the group would have most likely had a frustrating meeting with teachers talking past each other using the same language but meaning very different things.

If the group has read an article or chapter or collected student artifacts from their classrooms, the facilitator can help focus the discussion by encouraging members to share these as a way to begin discussion. Nothing is more frustrating to group members than to take time to read or to gather materials and not have them used or discussed. These readings or artifacts provide a common point for members and establish the issues that will focus the discussion. We found that when we did not begin with sharing these, the discussion took off in another direction and we never made it back to talking about the artifacts or reading. This was especially effective in the principal study group. When this group had difficulty staying on topic, reading a professional book or an article brought focus to the discussion.

Sometimes the discussion is exploratory as the group tries to determine the nature of the questions and what the members want to think more about. In some meetings, such as the one above on control and management, the group spent the entire session figuring out the questions members were really asking.

At other times the members have decided on a particular question and work at thinking through responses. The discussion constantly weaves between theory and practice as members consider classroom activities and the "why" behind those activities and their actions as teachers. The

Maldonado group was able to have this kind of discussion about class-room management at their next meeting. They decided their focus was on how to provide structures to support students in making productive decisions; this allowed the group to think through what those structures might be. Members also continuously asked themselves whether those structures facilitated learning or were only there to control behavior.

We found in some meetings that group members did not appear to be listening to each other or building on each other's comments. They were either intent on listing different activities or seemed to be sharing random thoughts related to the topic. In our role as facilitators, we asked reflective questions to encourage members to expand on their comments:

- "Talk about why you are doing that."
- "How is what you are doing different from_____?"
- "Could you explain what you mean by that?"
- "How does what you are doing relate to_____?"
- "Why would we do this in our classrooms?"
- "Why do/don't you like that book/activity?"

The "why" questions were especially important to extending and deepening the discussion. We also encouraged members to build on others' statements by engaging in those behaviors ourselves, "I agree with what Maria is saying. In my room, I noticed that . . ."

We did not expect the group to always stay on the topic. Momentary sidetracks are a normal part of any conversation. Our wait-time as facilitators greatly increased. Initially we immediately tried to bring the group back to the focus, but over time we realized that we needed to wait and see what would happen. Often the group brought itself back to the main focus after sharing several stories or pieces of information with each other. Other times, while the issue was off-topic, it was one the group quickly discussed before returning to the main focus. Still other times, what appeared to be a sidetrack allowed for a new perspective on the main focus. Being "on-task" every minute not only wasn't possible, it wasn't productive.

If the group did not return to the main topic of the meeting, we tried a range of strategies. One was to participate in the discussion by making a comment that connected back to the main focus to see if the rest of the group followed us (e.g., "Your comment reminds me of something that was in the article we read.") Another was a more direct route of pointing out that the group was on a sidetrack and asking if they wanted to remain there or asking "How does this issue relate to our main focus for today?" If the group chose to ignore our subtle or direct attempts at facilitating, we took that as a sign that they wanted to continue the discussion and we needed to back off.

Some groups consistently get off the main topic in their discussions. If the facilitator is unclear as to whether individual members are finding these many directions helpful, he or she can ask everyone to write a quick reflection at the end of the session in order to hear from each voice in the group. These reflections can then be the basis for a group discussion at the next meeting about whether to continue the off-topic talk.

If a group does want to work at staying on the topic, one possibility is to have the notetaker take notes for the meeting on a large visible chart so that everyone can see where the discussion is going. At the midpoint of the meeting, the notetaker could give a quick summary of the discussion so the group can refocus if necessary.

If the group is experiencing difficulty, it's also helpful at the end of the meeting for the facilitator to debrief with co-facilitators or a study group committee. They can talk about what happened during the meeting to figure out what went wrong and brainstorm strategies and structures that would be more supportive for the group's discussion.

Several of us are members of a study group on inquiry and sign systems. Since the members teach in many different school and university contexts, it was difficult to find a focus for our sessions, and we found ourselves staying at a sharing level. We tried several strategies that were effective in focusing our discussion. For a period of time, we read an article or chapter and used that as a point of focus. Then, each member agreed to write a short reflection or vignette related to the group's broad focus on inquiry and sign systems. Each person brought a one- to two-page free write to the meeting with copies for group members. The free writes were not revised or edited and so were not polished pieces of writing. They were very quick pieces of writing that group members spent fifteen minutes after school quickly pulling together. The reflections were on an event at school or in their lives or a professional reading or conference. The meeting began with everyone distributing and quietly reading the reflections. The group chose one of the reflections to start the conversation and moved from there to talking about the other reflections as they related to our discussion.

It is *not* the facilitator's responsibility to control the topic of discussion. Being "on task" is not defined as talking about the topic the facilitator believes should be discussed, but what members of the group want to discuss (and that often changes during a meeting). The goal of a study group is to construct new understandings about theory and practice, become more articulate about teaching, and question assumptions. There isn't a specific end point the group needs to reach.

Determining the Agenda

At the end of the meeting, the facilitator again plays a key role. If the members have been meeting in small groups, it's important to pull the small groups back together ahead of time so they can share the essence of their discussions with the whole group. Either the facilitator or the notetaker summarizes the highlights of the discussions and then the group negotiates the focus or issues for the next meeting. Other decisions, such as who will be the facilitator and notetaker are also discussed as well as the format, location, and time of the next meeting.

The Negotiation of the Agenda

The negotiation of the agenda involves determining the specific issues that a group wants to discuss related to the group's broad focus as well as the format, activities, methods, and schedule they will follow. When the Maldonado group selected student portfolios as their broad focus, the specific emphasis for one particular session was the types of items that could be put in a portfolio. Everyone agreed to bring examples from their classrooms. The schedule for that particular meeting consisted of sharing, breaking into small groups to look at the examples and create lists of possible items for portfolios, large-group sharing of these lists, reflection by the large group on related issues, and decisions on where to go next.

A study group makes these decisions about agenda through democratic processes at the end of each meeting. Group members plan the agenda together instead of one person making those decisions. Some groups found it helpful to have the notetaker quickly summarize or list the issues that were raised during the session. This quick listing provides a transition so that the group can reflect on that day's discussion and decide on their next focus. The facilitator encourages the group to think about whether to continue on the same issue, move on to a related issue, or completely change to a new focus.

As the facilitator, Kathy announced the transition to negotiating agenda by stating, "We're about out of time. What do you want to discuss at our next meeting? Are there other issues about this topic that you want to discuss or should we move on to something else?" Leslie facilitated this transition by stating, "We need to decide where this is going next time. Has everybody said what they wanted to say about today's topic?"

As the group considers where to go next in their discussion, we find that it is important to consider a range of ideas. Usually, group members are sitting on the edge of their chairs, ready to leave, and so it's easy to take the first suggestion even though that's not what everyone really wants to discuss. Everything is fine until the next meeting when the group is stuck with a focus that doesn't really interest them. By encouraging many suggestions and not just taking the first or loudest suggestion, members become more participatory and feel more ownership in the group. The facilitator can accept suggestions and encourage others to offer ideas by stating, "That's one idea to consider. What are some other possibilities? Who else has a suggestion?" When Leslie noticed that one table of teachers hadn't said much, she turned and asked, "Do you have any ideas to add? What do you think?" in order to invite their participation.

One member whose voice is sometimes given extra weight is the principal. We have found that group members tend to readily agree with suggestions offered by the principal, even though the principal is simply offering a possibility and isn't trying to impose a specific idea. The facilitator plays a particularly important role in acknowledging an idea and then asks for other suggestions or contributes another possibility if no one else speaks up right away.

We found that often we suggested options to encourage the group to be more specific and move ahead with a decision. By suggesting several options, we also invited members to add other possibilities. When the group was having difficulty deciding what they wanted to talk about as they moved into a new focus on portfolios, Kathy asked whether it made sense to start with reading several articles to get an overview of portfolios and their use or if they already had a good sense and wanted to get into specific issues. She did not push one of these options but simply offered them as a way to focus the decision process. In another instance, Clay asked the group, "What are we going to talk about next meeting?" When the group indicated that they wanted to stay with their current topic, he pushed them to be more specific, "Do you want to stay with the big issues of management and control or do you want to get into specifics?" This strategy of offering several possibilities was used frequently to facilitate the decision process so it didn't drag on forever.

We also found it helpful to select a particular focus that would last over several sessions. We would still need to make a decision on the specific issues we would discuss but the decision-making process didn't take as long. Whenever we needed to decide on a new broad focus for the group, more time was needed to make that decision.

Once the group has decided on a specific focus, then issues of format and appropriate activities are raised. For example, if a group is going to look at gender stereotypes in children's literature, they could decide to read a professional article or bring pieces of children's literature from their classrooms to examine for stereotypes. While the facilitator often has a larger role in suggesting a specific format for a particular session, we believe that topics and formats should be discussed and determined as much as possible by the group.

Sometimes a group member has a relevant article or chapter that the group can read. Since we met every other week, there was time to have copies made and put in everyone's mailboxes a week before our next meeting. Kathy initially made the mistake of bringing copies of an article with her to each meeting based on her prediction of where the group would go next. By doing so, she determined the next agenda and effectively stifled the negotiation. The group needed to negotiate the focus and *then* decide if there were relevant readings.

Sometimes the group decides to bring materials or student artifacts to the meeting or to engage in an experience before the next meeting. When the Warren group discussed field notes, everyone agreed to take some kind of field notes in their classroom before our next meeting. Some teachers took notes in a literature discussion group. Some followed a child for a day. Some took a lot of notes in a variety of contexts. Others took notes one day in one context. Everyone brought their notes to the next meeting and we started the meeting by sharing their different strategies for notetaking and then listing the issues and questions that were raised for further discussion.

At another time, the Warren study group had been discussing portfolios for several months. We had read various articles and chapters about different types of portfolios. We decided that we needed to put together some type of portfolio for our next meeting. Again, teachers made different decisions. Some had their entire class try a portfolio or had children write a self-evaluation of their learning. Some worked with one child to put together a portfolio. Some created a professional portfolio for themselves. Everyone brought these portfolios and we started out by sharing in small groups and then moved to a large-group discussion to share ideas and to list issues.

Sometimes the group brings in professional materials. When the Warren and Maldonado groups talked about mathematics and the move away from textbooks, they brought in professional books that were helpful in finding effective ways to use manipulatives in their classrooms. When the Warren group talked about literature circles, they agreed to bring in the children's books they had found successful in supporting children's discussions.

It isn't necessary that the group decide to read or bring something to the next meeting. Educators lead busy lives and aren't looking for something to do! Bringing an artifact to the meeting or reading an article does help to focus the discussion, but it can also produce tension for teachers who don't have time to follow through. They may feel that they cannot come if they haven't done their "homework." We find ourselves treading a thin line as we encourage everyone to read or try something and at the same time reassure group members that they should come whether or not they have completed the "homework."

In looking back at our group sessions, we realized that it is important that the decision to read or do something be a *group* decision, not a facilitator decision. In one session, Leslie asked the group, "What are *you* willing to do?" to clarify that this was their decision, not hers. In this case, the group wanted to read adult novels with multicultural themes and so had to work out what to read and how to get the books. Leslie refused to make the decisions for them and kept asking clarifying questions, "Where would we get the books?" "Who will get the books?" "How would we check them out?" "How will we prepare for the discussion?" These questions focused the group on the decisions they needed to make without putting Leslie in the position of deciding for them. She then summarized the decisions of the group to ensure that there was a common understanding.

We give ourselves "homework" only when we feel that the reading or activity is really needed so that our next session will be productive. We read about portfolios, for example, because many people didn't know what they were and we needed some kind of shared understanding. In at least half of our sessions, we simply agree on a topic, and group members go on their way without any special tasks to accomplish before the next meeting.

Whatever decisions the group does make should be summarized by the facilitator as the meeting ends so that everyone has a common understanding and agreement. As facilitator, Gloria ended the meeting by stating, "OK, so we're going to focus next week on the yearly plan by meeting in small groups first to share our plans and then move to a bigger group. So bring whatever you have done with your plans to share. Is that what everyone thinks we've agreed to do?"

We realize that it is not always possible to make all of these decisions at the end of a meeting. At the very least, the group needs to decide on the focus for the next meeting and whether they will do anything to prepare for that focus. The facilitator can propose a possible format, method, and schedule at the beginning of the next meeting.

Productive and Unproductive Agenda Topics

Of course, in our experiences with different groups, we have had sessions with both productive and unproductive topics for discussion. There are no guarantees for how an agenda will unfold during a meeting, even with the most careful negotiation of the topic. However, we have noted factors that affect the success of a focus.

Whenever agendas are unclear or uncertain, members of the study group tend to come unprepared or may even choose not to attend because there isn't a specific topic to engage their interest. As mentioned earlier, it's easy to rush off at the end of a meeting without clearly setting the next focus, but this creates tremendous difficulties for the next meeting. In our experience, deciding on a specific topic led to the best attendance and the most focused discussions in our groups. Members had time to consider the topic and often engaged in informal conversations with others before the group even met.

There are times when a group runs out of time and the meeting quickly ends without a decision. The facilitator is left in a difficult position of not wanting to determine the focus for the next session but with the realization that starting without a focus is usually unproductive because the group could spend the whole session trying to figure out their focus. Kathy handled this dilemma by going through the notes from the meeting and listing four possibilities based on the discussion. She started the next meeting by listing the four options and asking the group to quickly decide what they wanted to discuss.

Sometimes agendas are unclear because they are too broad. When the Maldonado group decided that they wanted to "talk about writing" at their next meeting, no one really knew what to discuss. A more specific topic—"What kinds of dialogue are productive during writing conferences?" or "What can go into a writing portfolio?"—was much more successful in supporting a focused discussion. Once we realized this, the facilitator began encouraging members to be more specific.

Additionally, it is crucial for members to have experiences and understandings of the topic. If the members have had little opportunity to read about a topic or work with that area of curriculum in their classrooms, then discussion may stall. When group members have a range of experiences related to the topic, the discussions are richer and many more members are involved. As we noted earlier, this appeared to be why our study group sessions about literature were much more productive than our discussions about mathematics. This does not mean that we should not have discussed mathematics but rather that when group members do not have experiences in their classroom with a topic, it may be more productive to start with discussion around a professional book that will allow shared understandings to develop. As Frank Smith (1988) notes, we need to know a lot about something in order to think critically about that topic.

One problem we ran into was selecting an agenda, not because it met our needs, but because we wanted to entice certain teachers to attend the group. The teachers who were the focus of our efforts resented our attempts to "fix" their teaching and the meetings became less productive for us. We realized that those of us who regularly attended the study group needed to make decisions based on what *we* needed, not on what we thought others who occasionally attended the group needed. We kept an invitation open to all school members but negotiated the agenda based on the needs and interests of the teachers present. The agenda of a study group is our own professional growth, not "fixing" the teaching of other educators in the school.

Changing the Broad Focus of the Group

Changing the group's broad focus occurs naturally when a topic has been exhausted through examination and discussion or the interests of the group members have changed. Sometimes a topic may not be completely exhausted, but attendance and participation are clearly indicating that it is no longer compelling for members. Other times, members feel overwhelmed by what has been discussed and need some time to live with the ideas in their classrooms before they discuss the topic further. At still other times, other topics are of greater interest or concern, and teachers are ready to move on.

When it becomes evident for any of these reasons that the time has come to change the focus of the group, the facilitator or another group member needs to raise the issue so the group can make a decision. If the group does decide to change their broad focus, they may want to come to some sort of closure by first reflecting on the experiences they have had with the current focus, and how that focus relates to the broad purpose of the group. The group may then want to revisit their original brainstorming chart and make additions to that list before discussing alternatives for where they might go next. When the Maldonado group finished their focus on math, they went back to their original brainstorming, added to it, and realized that writing was a theme that kept coming up. Many of them had worked at various types of writing workshops for a number of years and wanted to revisit what was happening. Also, they could continue the math focus by examining writing about mathematical concepts.

Throughout the process, the facilitator should encourage the group to consider as many ideas as possible before making a decision. We found over and over again that it's far too easy to settle on the first idea that sounds good. Whenever we acknowledged those good ideas but kept adding others, we ended up with a far more generative topic, and we thought about more complex issues because of the negotiation process.

Who Should Facilitate the Group?

While we all agree that the choice of facilitator is an extremely important decision, our experiences indicate that no one decision is the right one. We have been involved in a range of successful groups that made very different decisions about the facilitator. Sometimes the facilitator is an outside person who is not a member of that school. Other times the facilitator comes from within the school. Sometimes the same person serves as the facilitator for each meeting. Other times the facilitator role rotates between some or all of the group members.

Bringing in an Outside Facilitator

There are several reasons why an outside facilitator might be a good choice for a particular group. Sometimes the relationships within a particular school are so difficult that an experienced facilitator is needed in order to effectively deal with interpersonal dynamics. In schools where teachers have divided themselves into different factions, choosing someone within that school can be seen as "showing favorites" or "choosing sides." Even in cases where there aren't major interpersonal problems, a teacher moving into the role of facilitator can violate school norms and seem to establish a hierarchy where one teacher has authority over others resulting in professional jealousy.

Sometimes the issue isn't divisive relationships, but the fact that no one in the school has ever been part of a study group. An outside facilitator who is familiar with a study group format can introduce that format to the school and help get the group established. Teachers within the school can then continue with the group on their own.

Another reason for choosing an outside facilitator is when the group wants to discuss a topic that is unfamiliar or uncomfortable to the group. In that case, they may need the support of a facilitator who is knowledgeable in that area and can provide support in terms of professional materials and information, and help define underlying issues. The key concern in this case is the problem of that person dominating the group and turning the group into an inservice presentation.

Kathy served as an outside facilitator for the Warren/Maldonado and the Warren study groups for several years because of her interest in study groups. She wanted to experience whether or not study groups would be an effective form of professional development. While she had experience facilitating other kinds of groups, she had not been part of a study group before and neither had the teachers in these two buildings. As teachers became familiar with the study group process, they were more willing to take over the role of facilitator.

One of the advantages Kathy had as an outside facilitator was that she was not part of the past history of social and professional relationships in the school. She could observe and facilitate difficult situations without having other motivations attached to her actions. On the other hand, she sometimes facilitated in inappropriate ways because she didn't know the history and misread a particular interaction. She found that her wait-time greatly increased through this experience. She didn't step into the discussion to facilitate as quickly but waited longer to see where the conversations might go.

Kathy found that having an established expertise in the area under discussion, literature-based curriculum, was both an advantage and a disadvantage. On the one hand, she had access to many resources that could support issues that came up for discussion. She could also often move the discussion from practical ideas to deeper theoretical issues as well as offer specific practical ideas for concerns that came up. She suggested possible directions for discussions that might not have been considered without her presence.

On the other hand, her expertise got in the way because it led many in the group to expect an inservice model. They were more interested in hearing her speak than in learning how to think and dialogue with each other. At one point, several members came to her and said, "We want to know what you know. We want to hear what you have to say." Kathy felt that it took longer for group members to come to value each other and the process of dialogue because of her presence. These pressures from group members sometimes led her to dominate more of the talk time than she intended.

One of her strategies to move out of the expert role and still participate in the group was by sharing her own teaching "story" (Short, 1992). She shared personal examples and stories instead of making general statements about "what research says." She gave a specific example from her own teaching or from her interactions in someone else's room. Sharing in this way allowed what she said to appear less as "truth" and more as an idea for others to consider. She made comments such as, "I remember the year I first moved to literature-based curriculum and I had nightmares about whether what I was doing was all right." or "A teacher that I worked with in Goshen had a student who engaged in similar behaviors, and she tried several strategies." She carefully used phrases such as "I've noticed" or "I've found" rather than "You should" or "You need to" as she responded in discussions.

Another strategy to get beyond the expert designation was to suggest references and resources that group members could explore so they didn't see Kathy as the only source. She also suggested a range of options in response to a specific question instead of giving one answer. Finally, she often referred questions to teachers in the group who were working on that issue in their own classrooms. This strategy was especially important to creating an environment in which everyone shared their expertise.

When the district wanted to encourage schools to offer study groups as an option, it offered to provide outside facilitators to any school that wanted to begin a group. During the fall, ten to twelve teachers and resource personnel who were interested in becoming facilitators met in a study group on study groups. They then served as outside facilitators in schools who were interested in starting a study group during the spring. This effort met with mixed success, mostly because of the difficulty of arranging for an outside facilitator to come from another school in the district.

Over time, most schools moved to having teachers within the building serve as facilitators. In addition, once principals became involved in the principal study group, many encouraged the formation of teacher study groups in their buildings because they valued the dialogue occurring in their own group. They did not serve as facilitators but provided support and made arrangements so that the groups could form and meet.

Having a Group Member Serve as Facilitator

We have all served as facilitators in study groups in our own teaching contexts. One major issue is balancing the role of being both an observer/ reflector and a participant. In the first role, we assess how the group is working by stepping back from the group process, looking at the group, and offering comments that facilitate the talk and open it up to more voices. As participants, we join in the conversations and offer our thoughts and listen to the reactions of others to help us articulate our own ideas. The participant role is important to us because we initially joined the group in order to learn as teachers. However, when we get too involved as participants, we miss opportunities to facilitate the group.

In the roles of facilitator and participant, we offer comments to which people respond, and at the same time step back as observers and continue to facilitate. The transition from participant to observer and back again is a quick one and can cause initial discomfort when one takes more of a leadership role with colleagues. Most of us did not have previous experience with facilitating the talk of other adults. Depending on the traditions that have developed within a school in terms of how teachers relate to each other, this shift can be a major one. It is less striking in schools where teachers have always taken a variety of leadership roles including leading staff meetings, presenting at inservices, etc.

Serving as facilitators in our own schools made us somewhat vulnerable and put us up for evaluation by others who could critique what we were doing. Particularly when we were new at facilitation, there were moments of doubt and uncertainty about what we were doing, and there were times when we made mistakes. Some of us were more successful than others in our initial attempts. However, as more and more teachers tried their hand at facilitation, the study group strengthened because each member recognized how to make facilitative comments whether or not the individual was in the official role of facilitator. Gradually, the facilitation was shared among group members. As we examined transcripts, we noted other members asking questions for clarification, restating what someone had said, acknowledging someone's comment, and encouraging group members to extend their comments through "why" questions.

We saw a number of advantages to teachers serving as their own facilitators. One was the ease of scheduling. Another was the professional growth that each person experienced as they learned how to handle group dynamics. This experience carried over into our own classrooms as well as into our relationships with each other. We learned *how* to talk in productive ways with each other, instead of becoming dependent on someone else to facilitate our talk. Learning to acknowledge differences of opinion as facilitators led to an atmosphere of greater respect and openness among the staff itself.

Still another advantage was that we brought an internal knowledge of the people in that building. We had been in each other's classrooms and had spent time living and talking with the study group members both personally and professionally. We shared a knowledge of district mandates and the ways in which the school was run. We were aware of relationships among the staff. Suggestions that we offered as a way to transition the group to a new topic or within the same topic reflected the history we had with our colleagues.

This understanding of relationships can support talk in a variety of ways, particularly in decisions of whether to invite conflict or avoid counterproductive confrontations. When particular members shared opinions that were in direct opposition to each other, we used our knowledge of staff history to make a split-second decision of whether to diffuse the situation or encourage the discussion.

One difficulty in facilitating talk within our own schools is that sometimes we know too much about particular individuals and try to second guess their responses. We also sometimes worry too much about how other people will react to what we are saying or doing as facilitators and become self-conscious. It can be intimidating and challenging to reveal ourselves in a different light to other staff members.

Exploring Other Options for the Facilitator Role

There are a number of variations we have explored relative to the facilitator role and to the length of time any one person should serve in that role. In some cases, the same person has served as facilitator for each meeting. This option has worked well in cases where someone in the school is an experienced and effective facilitator or where other group members are reluctant or unable to take on that responsibility. Having the same facilitator over time provides continuity from meeting to meeting. However, it also means that one person is handling a great deal of responsibility, and the group can come to be seen as that person's group instead of a shared community of educators. Also no one else develops experience at facilitating.

In other cases, the role of the facilitator rotates among group members. Not everyone has to take on the role, but group members are encouraged to consider the role. We found that it worked well to not necessarily change the facilitator at every meeting, especially if the group was discussing a particular topic over two or three meetings. In that case, we asked the same person to stay as facilitator for that set of meetings and as soon as the group moved on to a new topic, someone else became the facilitator.

A related option is to have a small group of people who agree to rotate the role of facilitator among themselves. Sandy and Leslie were part of a team of three at their current school. Such an arrangement gives continuity without putting all of the responsibility on one person.

Sometimes there is a logical group of people to serve as facilitators. Kathy worked with a districtwide language arts committee that had been talking and reading the professional literature on literature-based curriculum for two years. As the district moved toward a new adoption, the committee decided to start study groups in each school with the two to three members of the committee from that school serving as the facilitators.

Another variation we have tried is to have co-facilitators at each meeting. The two facilitators share the responsibility for the meeting and are able to plan and debrief with each other. This type of arrangement encourages teachers who would be reluctant to facilitate the group by themselves, but are willing to co-facilitate with someone else.

Using a Committee to Support the Facilitator

At Warren, we decided one person should not have all of the responsibilities for organizing and facilitating the study group. Because teachers serve on committees to conduct the work of that school, forming a committee to support the study group was a natural way for us to work together. Sandy, Leslie, and Barb served on this committee when it was first formed. The committee had three major duties—to prepare written announcements and organize the notes from the meetings, to address logistical issues of time and place, and to provide support for whoever was serving as facilitator for a particular meeting. The committee oversaw the work of the study group and provided continuity for the facilitator and the group members.

One task of the committee was to distribute notes to everyone a few days prior to the next meeting. These notes briefly summarized the previous meeting, listed continuing questions, described the agenda for the next meeting, and listed the facilitator as well as the dates and times.

The summary was given by the notetaker to a committee member. The actual notes taken during the meeting were put in a committee notebook. We found that while the facilitator took notes during the meeting to remember points relevant to the current session, the notetaker took notes with future conversations in mind. The notes included summative comments as well as unresolved questions. The committee kept the notes in a notebook along with announcements to provide a public record of what was going on in the meeting.

The committee also set up the room for the meeting. This usually involved moving the tables into a circle and bringing in chairs. We set up the room so we could easily meet in both small and large groups as needed. The committee established where and when each session would take place and met with the principal to determine meeting dates.

The committee also supported the facilitator, as this person was usually not a member of the committee. Before each study group meeting, the committee met with the facilitator and brainstormed possible topics and questions related to the focus, as well as possible ways of organizing the meeting. In addition, the committee met with the facilitator immediately after the session to examine the direction that the discussion had gone and to analyze group dynamics as well as discuss issues that had been raised related to the topic for the meeting.

Conclusion

The facilitator role is a challenging one, requiring a great deal of risk-taking and experience; but the effort is well worth the risk. Not only is facilitating important to the success of a study group, but the strategies learned carry over into other staff interactions and into the classroom.

For teachers who are attempting to create a learning-centered classroom, it's a critical step. We found that taking on this role influenced the way in which we thought about our teaching. We were able to move to more collaborative curricula, where teachers and students shifted roles, depending on expertise, needs, and interests. As teachers, we found ourselves taking the facilitator role into our classroom learning environments—we shared, rather than presented, and established credibility along with vulnerability. Our focus moved from control to inquiry. Problems were not "bad" or "wrong," but questions and issues that needed to be addressed and possibilities we wanted to understand and explore.

We believe that educators need to experience the same type of learning environment that students need—a place where we can be inquirers and ask questions that matter in our lives. Many of us had never experienced learning in an environment with a facilitator. We needed to "live the process" both as a learner and as a facilitator in order to connect this process with our own teaching. The facilitator role is thus not only essential to the functioning of the study group itself, but for the broader implications of how we think of ourselves as teachers.

The following guidelines provide a quick summary of the facilitator's role and can be used as a reference by facilitators during meetings:

Guidelines for Facilitators

1. Make a plan for proposed agenda along with back-up plans and options

- Think ahead. Consider possible directions the discussion could take and the most appropriate format for discussion.

- If discussion falls apart, *suggest* stand-by plans, but don't impose those plans.

2. Actively direct beginning of meeting

- Begin with 15–20 min. of sharing.

- Start meeting on time by inviting members to share.

- Briefly summarize previous meeting with outline of that day's agenda.

- As sharing ends, restate topic and suggest format, particularly whether to have small groups.

- Suggest a change in agenda if a major issue has been raised in sharing.

- Ask the group to quickly list important issues related to the topic of the meeting.

- Begin by discussing readings or sharing artifacts previously agreed upon by the group.

3. During meeting, facilitate discussion and encourage members to share their perspectives

- Be an "active listener."

- Help members "hear" each other by restating unacknowledged statements.

- Open discussion to new voices, be aware of whose voice is not being heard, or what is not being said but needs to be said.

- Invite elaboration and clarification.

- If group is off topic, make sure that they are aware of that choice.

- Encourage group to connect theory and practice by looking for the bigger issues behind specific activities or problems.

- Offer a procedure to resolve heated debates rather than take a stand.

- Enter the discussion as a participant, but remember to pull back to observe and facilitate.

4. Negotiate agenda at the end of the meeting

- Move from discussion to negotiation 15 minutes from the ending time.

- Remind group about issues raised but not addressed during meeting.

- Summarize highlights of discussion.

■ Facilitate negotiation of new agenda, format, facilitator, notetaker, location for next meeting.

■ Decide as a group how to prepare for the next meeting (readings, classroom experiences, etc.)

■ Facilitate these decisions, ask for suggestions, and mention possible options, but do not make decisions for the group.

5. Responsibilities after the meeting

■ Distribute notes from meeting or ensure they are distributed by the notetaker.

■ Notes should be a summary of the meeting and an invitation to attend the next meeting.

■ Notes should inform members about next agenda topic and identify the facilitator, location, and date of next meeting.

5 What Does a Study Group Session Sound Like?

One of the questions that we are frequently asked is "What really goes on in a study group session?" We realize that those asking this question are trying to envision the way in which a session develops and the kinds of conversation that occur. We also know that the questioners don't expect all study group sessions to be the same but need a vision for what a study group might look and sound like in order to see the possibilities within their own settings. In this chapter, we have included excerpts from an actual study group session as an attempt to provide that vision. No study group session is "typical" but this one does give a sense of our experiences in the study group.

The study group session in which we are inviting you to participate occurred in April during the second year of the Warren study group. The group had been talking about literature circles and decided to focus on field notes as a way to evaluate what was happening in the discussions. We had discussed field notes the previous year as part of a focus on evaluation, but had primarily talked about types of notes and strategies for taking notes. To prepare, everyone agreed to take field notes of a discussion and to bring those notes with them to the meeting. Our notes were anecdotal records where we quickly scripted students' talk or wrote down observations of their behaviors.

We edited this transcript, in particular taking out the "you knows" and stammerings that are part of oral speech. We interspersed the transcript with our own commentary, which is indicated in italics. This particular meeting was attended by seven primary teachers, six intermediate teachers, the librarian, the principal (Myna Matlin), and Kathy as the facilitator.

Warren Study Group
April 9

Kathy: Does anybody have something they want to share before we get started?

Leslie: Last time we talked about books to use in literature groups. This book, *Twenty and Ten,* is a book that I've seen as a read aloud in as low as grade three. It's not difficult. It's about the Holocaust and twenty Christian children take in ten Jewish children. And it's that whole conflict of not only where they're going to hide them, but the issue of loyalty and not betraying and being afraid and coping with that and problem solving. Kids really like the book.

Manuel: Yeah, but the kids don't have that concept. You ask the kids about this and they'll say, "Well, we'd go to the mountains and hide." I said "For four-and-a-half years?" You know, they don't really understand what it would take to survive. I said "What would happen if I took two kids to Mt. Lemmon and left you there? You'd die."

Leslie: Yeah, this kid in my room said, "Well, if I went back in time, I would kill Hitler." He doesn't have the concept that he's not omnipotent. He's just a boy. And even as a boy in our society he can't do something like that either; but they think they can do anything.

Karen: I wonder if that's their way of dealing with the powerlessness that kids face. You know, "I can do it." They know that that's not a possibility, but they don't want to think that they couldn't do anything.

Leslie: Yeah. I've thought about if I had been around during the Holocaust and it happened to me, would I survive?

Manuel: Well you never think it's going to happen to you; but it really happens.

Leslie: I have to think that a lot of my family who didn't survive were just as strong as I am. And I got a letter recently from somebody in my mother's family's hometown who's writing a book about what happened to the Jews there. He wrote that my grandmother went to a concentration camp and died of weakness. And I thought to myself, "Died of weakness! What nonsense!"

Karen: You know I just read this allegory for the Holocaust about animals and the "terrible thing." First they came for the birds and the little rabbit said, "Shouldn't we do something?" and all the other rabbits said, "No, we're not birds; don't worry." And then slowly, but surely the bad thing comes for each group of animals until only the rabbits are left. And the little rabbit's still saying, "Shouldn't we do something?" and then it's too late. I just discovered that book and it had a 1972 copyright date. It's just been republished because nobody will publish the book because it's so upsetting to adults. I think it's so exciting that you're talking about it.

Kathy: Does anyone else have anything to share? [Silence]

Kathy: We decided to talk about field notes today and people were going to bring field notes from a literature discussion. Do you want to start out talking about issues based on your experiences and then spend some time looking at field notes and how to analyze them? ["Yes" murmurs] What kinds of issues do you want to raise about field notes?

———

Kathy's question was a signal to the group that it was time to move into the main focus but that there was still time if someone had something important to share. When no one responded, she reminded the group of their focus on taking and analyzing field notes of literature discussions and suggested a possible format for the discussion. She proposed starting with issues to get a sense of what the group might find productive to discuss.

———

Leslie: Let's talk about how hard they are to take. [Laughter]

Barb: Do the older children talk as fast as the little teeny ones? [Laughter]

James: Probably faster.

Barb: I don't think I've ever heard a group talk as fast as that first grade group did today. They talked so fast, I got maybe a third down of what they were saying.

Pat: Yeah. What do you do?

Barb: I couldn't write fast enough. I can't always tell who all the students are who are talking.

Anne: Well, just get the conversation, not the names.

Barb: No, I want the names, that's the whole point.

Kathy: Normally what I do is write their names across the top and then I only use an initial. Like if it's Carl and Susan and Anita, then I just use a "C" and an "S" and an "A".

Margaret: I put the names at the top so I know and then write down just whatever I can get of the conversation.

Anne: Then that doesn't give you time to really listen and enjoy what they're saying. You're too busy.

Pat: I get so involved in what's going on that I forget to take notes.

Anne: You need a third person there just to take notes.

Kathy: I think it's really hard right now just because it's new.

Sharon: If you want to say something to take them to a different level, it really helps to have all of those words down. It helps you in what you're going to say to them. If you're going to take them from one place to another. It would really help me to be able to do it well so that I would be able to know what to say to them.

Pat: I noticed Kathy will repeat and kind of help them to refocus on what they've said. I mean, it's there in her notes and she can read it off and help them refocus and move a level.

Sharon: It also helps if you write down what you're asking, like "What went well or what didn't go well?"

Kathy: Yeah, I just put a "T" and whatever my question was because it changes the conversation when you do that.

Karen: Sharon, I have a question about what you said. I think what I heard is if you want to take kids to a higher level or a different perspective, it's easier to have their words in front of you so that you can start from there.

Sharon: I'm talking about levels of thinking. So, if they were having this conversation about this book and I wanted to help them get to another level of thinking, if I have all of their words written down, then I know exactly what they said and I can think in my mind what I'm going to say to them since I know exactly what they said.

Karen: What is it that you're using to make the decisions then? About what you're going to say?

Sharon: Their words. The thinking was coming out of their head. And so if I have it written down so that I know exactly where it is and then I don't forget it.

Kathy: Like today when I was in her room, her kids were talking about *Pinkerton Behaves*, and a couple of them said that this is not a bedtime story. I was curious about their criteria. And so I said "Why are you saying that?" I guess it was a teacher judgment in terms of looking where there's a potential.

Anne: What did they answer back?

Leslie: And look, she's showing us how to use field notes by finding it. What a good facilitator. [Laughter]

Kathy: Thank you, Leslie. The positive reinforcement was wonderful. Here it is: "My mom says that when stories are too rough, it winds you up and you can't sleep. They're too rowdy." Then the other boy said, "This book is mostly about morning and there's only a little part of it that's about night. And it's too scary because there's a burglar and it's scary because of how threatened he gets." (See example, p. 84.)

Anne: I wonder if they're comparing that to stories they are read to at night? Or do the families say, "You can't watch that movie because it's too violent," or both?

Kathy: But the little girl said, "My mom said stories." She and her mother had a discussion about what she could and could not read. And the little boy, it was more that he was thinking on his own about why he thought this book wasn't a bedtime story.

Sharon: He was the one who said we needed to talk about whether it was a bedtime story or whether it was a just-for-fun story.

Kathy: Yeah. And then later he said that he can sleep with silly stories. He can read silly stories before he goes to sleep and he'll laugh in his sleep. He said, "My mom read me about Amelia Bedelia having overalls and I still slept well." [Laughter]

Kathy: Leslie, what did you mean by "How hard it is?" I mean, is there something specific that you're trying to do or is it getting used to it or what?

————

Note that in this discussion of issues, Kathy, as the facilitator, participated as a member of the group, sharing her experiences as the group thought through a problem. Also note that other group members used facilitative talk, as for example when Karen asked Sharon to clarify what she said. Karen's question about how Sharon makes these decisions is a good example of a question that helps participants connect practice and theory. Sharon described a practice and Karen wanted to understand the "why" of that practice. However, it's also important to know that these two members had a personal conflict and that was one reason Kathy offered an example to support Sharon's comment.

At this point, a pause in the discussion made it clear that the group was finished with that topic, so Kathy asked a question about an earlier issue that Leslie had raised. She wanted to ensure that Leslie's concerns weren't overlooked by the group and to give Leslie a chance to clarify her point. She also saw this as a good opportunity to take the group back to the focus on field notes. Note that she did not talk after asking the clarifying question of Leslie because she wanted to give

③

A: dog tore report card, got rid of burglar

S: dogs should be trained. My dog is learning
   slowly and does bad things

R: story is just for fun; not a bedtime story

B: too rowdy for bedtime

T: Why?

B: My mom says that when stories are too
   rough, it winds you up and you can't sleep.
   They're too rowdy

R: This book is mostly about morning and there's
   only a little part of it that's about night.
   It's scary because there's a burglar and it's
   scary because of how threatened he gets

A: is a bedtime story — when I read it, I get
   sleepy; have to wake up and read it

S: feel bad for Pinkerton; does everything wrong

F: don't like page with guns; not to touch guns
   so don't like page

A: look how big he is (shows picture of real dog
   on back corner)
Group examines picture & talks about size
P: Burglar is scared of him

Example of Field Notes.

the group space in order to take the discussion in a different direction if they chose. However, she didn't want to impose that topic, and the group was free to ignore the direction she was suggesting with her question.

Leslie: Part of it, I guess, is getting used to writing that fast. I'm not really used to getting down exactly what they're saying. I'm more used to summarizing it and putting down phrases and so that's really what I'm doing; but I can't quote that well. I know I tend to analyze it as I'm writing it. I'll write it and then I'll put a comment on the side. Then my brain is split three ways because I'm writing and I'm thinking and I'm listening to them. It *really* is difficult for me. It gets even harder.

Karen: Is it hard later on to decipher what the kids are saying from your own comments?

Leslie: No, because I do it visually on a very specific part of the page. I put it in parentheses or brackets so that I know it's my thought. And also, of course, sometimes you really want to participate in the conversation. It's a good monitor because if you say something then you need to write it down so you see where the conversation goes and how it got there. Sometimes I really have ideas that I want to say and it just keeps me in check—not to say nothing, but to say a little something and not take it over. I also took field notes in math and that was very helpful because I asked the kids what they thought fractions were. And I could look at it later and really know what they knew. I can't necessarily do it with literature yet, but it was so clear to me by looking at the field notes that they have some gross misconceptions about fractions.

Manuel: Isn't it a lot easier to have a tape recorder because you know the kids' voices anyway and you could play it.

Barb: I've tried taping and I don't always recognize voices, and I've missed taping some things that I wanted. Sometimes it's hard with little ones and they don't remember who they are.

Manuel: But when you call the person's name. You can make that part of the tape.

Margaret: But what you're trying to do is take notes of *their* discussion. You don't want to be that much a part of it.

Manuel: I know you're not going to be talking all the time. But see like Leslie's asking the kids about fractions. She could say, "_____what's your definition of a fraction?"

Laura: But then you'd have led the discussion, Manuel.

Manuel: Yeah, you're leading it.

Laura: As soon as you start to say "What's your . . ."

Manuel: Well she's leading the discussion anyway.

Margaret: No, you're not! That's not my goal.

Barb: I didn't lead the discussion with the first graders today. I didn't do anything but listen and write as fast as I could write. They were talking about wishing wells because we read that story and I was listening to them talk about it. And it was really interesting, the dialogue going back and forth about wishing wells. And they asked each other if they believed it and I didn't have to ask them anything. They just got on the topic and ran away with it and I couldn't write fast enough.

Manuel: But you brought it about, right? You're the one that mentioned the wishing wells before the discussion started.

Barb: No, they read a story.

Manuel: So then you just sat back and said, "What do you think of wishing wells?"

Barb: No. I didn't say anything. All I did was give each group their story and said, "This is what we're going to have a test on. I want you to handle this as though it was a literature study. I want you to read it. And then I want you as a group to discuss things about your story." And I had three different stories going because I have three different grade levels. And I was trying to go from grade level to grade level to see what the different ones were talking about, but I wasn't leading the discussion. The story wasn't actually about "Do you believe in wishing wells?" It was a make-believe story about this wishing well that said "Ouch!" when somebody threw a penny in it. They got into issues with each other. Veronica is the first one that asked someone "Do you believe in wishing wells?" So I never had to say anything. But I couldn't write fast enough.

This discussion about a teacher's role in a literature discussion is a slight side-track from the main focus on field notes but the group saw it as an important issue to pursue. These sidetracks were a common characteristic of study group discussions. Note that Barb brought the group back to the focus on field notes with her last comment. The test that Barb mentioned was a district assessment on reading comprehension that everyone in the school was administering during that week.

This discussion is also a good example of teachers challenging each other in a positive manner. Manuel's question was a genuine one and the others responded to him in a serious and thoughtful way.

———————

Kathy: I summarize and get down phrases or if everybody is saying "I like," then I might write "I like" and put a list underneath it of what each person says.

Barb: But I really do wish I had taped that conversation because it was so spontaneous for some reason and someone in the group just sparked it and they just took off.

Kathy: The people in my literature discussion class who taped listened to the tape in the car. And some people taped when they couldn't be at a group. They said that when the tape recorder was running, the group thought it was more serious and focused on the discussion more.

Barb: Well, that's one of the things I wanted to ask because I've thought about doing tape recorders to help the children know that this isn't play time. You're supposed to really be doing it. Does it work?

Leslie: It works, I think, for a certain amount of time. And then I still think that if you don't process in the class later, they won't believe it. Because if you don't listen to the tape and actually come back to them at some point and say, "You know, I heard you say such and such the other day while I was listening to your tape," they think it's just for nothing and you're pulling their leg.

Barb: Well, more than likely I would probably type it out on the computer. And ask the kids to come over if I don't know who said it so I would have a transcript.

Leslie: Well, you know, in a lot of cases that's fabulous; but my time is really incredibly limited and to transcribe a tape is a phenomenal process. It takes an *incredible* amount of listening and *time*.

Barb: But it saves you time in other ways. I spend a lot of time writing things down in portfolios. And it would be nice to have that dialogue and just be able to cut the strips and put them in each child's portfolio.

Becky: The mistakes took me forever to correct. Do you think I'm going to type it all up again? I can't imagine it.

Karen: You have to show kids there's an audience. It's like when kids feel that they are writing for a basket—when they get done with their writing, they put it in the basket and nobody ever reads it again.

Barb: I used to write little notes and stick it on there and then later on I would write it out so I wouldn't forget them.

Leslie: Well, that's what I'm doing with field notes. I mean that's what I'm *trying* to do. I'm trying to just keep them in one place and not lose them. That's the hard part for me. Because I keep thinking most of the notes aren't anything and then I throw them out. [Laughter]

Karen: Well, I was taking dictation today and Elena wouldn't say another word until I looked up at her. Then she'd say one word and when she saw my pencil stop, she'd say the next word.

Leslie: But you know I have actually found that whole processing time at the end of literature groups to be really important. What happens is the kids reflect on what they've said. They go back a little bit and they reflect on what they've said and if they've seen anything really new. It's just an avenue where they can talk about it to the class and spark other kids to think in different ways. I did a practice of how that reflection would look by reading *Dawn* by Molly Bang and then they talked about it and I listened and had them tell me aloud some of the things they said. And then I read it again. I did it in a different color of pen on a different acetate sheet and showed them what they said, and how their responses got deeper into the book. And how their connections were broader. And that also helps, just that modeling so that when they're sitting in groups, a *lot* of the kids will say, "Well, you know, yes, it was a really weird book." At first the kids said *Dawn* was a weird story and this boy said, "It's just a weird story and I know that the author made it up because well maybe his wife left him. Maybe the father was telling the girl because the wife left him and he wanted to explain it and so he put it into a fairy tale for her." You know he just couldn't get really past that idea. But then other kids saw a variety of different things in it. The other part is that not only the conversation gets deeper, but you can bring in your own thinking. Because I said to them, "Does this have anything to do with the Holocaust?" just as a question. I was trying to elicit their responses so when they go back to the literature discussions, they're more experienced at talking in depth.

Leslie's comments about how she worked at getting greater depth of thinking in literature groups connected back to Sharon's earlier discussion of this issue. Obviously Leslie has continued to think about that issue even though the group moved on. While her comments initially seem to be off-topic, she went on to share how she used field notes to support her efforts to help kids move to deeper thinking. She talked about what she does with field notes and why they are of value to her. Her focus was on why she takes notes rather than on how she does it.

Sharon: Did you ever have groups of children listening to other groups of children who were discussing? [Question to facilitator]

Kathy: Like a fish bowl? I haven't done that, but I know other people who have. They gather a small group in the middle and the other kids sit around the outside and listen to get a sense of what literature groups are all about. I don't like being in a fish bowl when people have done that to me and so I don't do it with kids. It's just uncomfortable for me. But I know other teachers who use it and really like the strategy. And then they process with the whole class, "What did they notice about this discussion? How did it go? What was said?" So they use it in a similar way to what Leslie was just talking about.

Barb: I probably do lead the discussion more than I don't lead it. Today I didn't have to. It just happened.

Kathy: But if it's collaborative you should be able to lead sometime. Just not all the time.

In this case, Sharon looked to Kathy as an expert and Kathy responded by sharing her perspective but did not give a definite answer. Instead, she shared different sides of the issue and tied her comments back to Leslie's earlier comments about her processing time with literature groups.

Karen: I've been taking a different kind of role because I didn't establish a situation where we're in group discussions yet because we're focusing on Bill Peet. I've been keeping a running tally of comments that are the spontaneous comments of kids. When we come to a discussion, I have the kids keep a record. We haven't had a discussion yet because they're working to read the stories. I record the things they notice as I read to them or they read. My intention is to have each child or pair of children become an expert on a single book and we'll all become experts on something and compare those first and then look at those themes that run through many of his books. That's still a form of field notes.

Kathy: Yeah, the kind of notes you take depend on what it is you're trying to find out. So it's going to be widely varied.

Karen: I started it by accident because of one kid who noticed the same car in several books. I thought "Well, I guess I should keep track."

―――――――

Karen's comments brought the group back to the focus on field notes. Kathy's comment is a restatement that summarized what Karen said and related it to the broader issue that there are many different options for how to take field notes.

―――――――

Kathy: I was just thinking as you were talking about another use. Kathleen [who had previously been a member of the group] was doing these groups on the desert and she taped all the groups. She decided to take a look at this one group of four boys that seemed to be a total flop. She transcribed it and noticed that she was being too hard on them. They were actually saying things that she had missed just listening to the group in the classroom. But then she noticed that they started out saying "First we're going to do the mural and then the second thing we're going to do is the book." And Kathleen says, "Do you remember what we talked about yesterday?" "Yeah." "About how you guys were going to talk about the book." "Yeah." They were so into projects that she couldn't get them to talk about the books. And then she noticed that they'd each ask questions but nobody listened to anybody else. The next person would ask their question. And so what she did with this transcript was she took it back to the group. She read it to this group of first graders. And then they discussed what they heard and they saw right away that they were asking lots of questions and nobody was responding. In fact one little boy said "Yeah, I asked my question and nobody listened to me at all so I just didn't talk anymore." So they came up with this strategy where they'd ask all their questions and get them written down and then they'd choose one of those. Because they were afraid that if they didn't ask them, they'd forget it. They'd talk about one question and then they'd come back and get another one.

But it was real interesting to see how the field notes or, in this case, a transcript, was used with the kids. She did go back through later and label what kind of talk each statement seemed to be, like if it was an opinion or about a character or an evaluation. She created a list of her own categories. She wanted some way to evaluate the literature groups and so she would take the transcript or notes and off to the side write down the kind of talk. She had a checklist with all the kids' names and then at the top she would write whichever categories of talk seemed the most appropriate to look for at that time. And then she'd read through the field notes, and whenever the kids were talking about that, she'd check it off. So she had an evaluation sheet to give her a sense of the range of things kids discussed in the group. And it wasn't that they had to discuss all of the categories, but she could see the patterns of discussion and see which children were talking—maybe only doing retellings and never contributing any other kind of talk in the groups.

Laura: I want to go back to something. Barb, when you gave the test to your kids, what did you say? How did you do it?

———————

Kathy shared an experience with another teacher, Kathleen, as a way to build on what both Leslie and Karen had shared. This experience was another example of how teachers might use field notes, further addressing the issue of "Why take field notes?" What's interesting is that Laura's question ignored what Kathy shared and looped back to Barb's earlier comments that Laura had obviously been thinking about ever since. Everyone had to give the district test that week, so this issue was an immediate concern. Laura saw Barb as a resource for a way to approach the test with her own students.

———————

Barb: I told them that we were going to be tested and I showed them the tests. I read a few of the questions and gave them a general idea of what was expected from the tests. And then they each got their literature book and I said, "I want you to do this as you would any other literature study. Read the stories the way you normally do and then discuss them. And when you are finished, I'll pass out the tests."

Laura: Did you break them up into groups or did they just make their own groups or what?

Barb: They made their own groups. In a couple of instances I changed them, but they basically made their own groups.

Laura: I was trying to think how I would do that in my class.

Barb: I didn't give them any criteria to make their groups; they're used to mixing them. But one group was going to be just boys and I said, "You know, you need to have a couple of girls in your group."

Rena: They'd finished reading it and they were talking about it, but you didn't hand out the tests yet, did you?

Barb: They started them *after* their discussion.

Manuel: How many groups did you have at the same time? [*Barb:* Six.] And they were all discussing the same story?

Barb: No. They had three different books for the three different grade levels in my classroom. [Note: Barb teaches a multi-age primary class.]

Myna: But if it were all one grade, they'd all be given the same book.

Barb: Right. They'd all be using the same book because of the fact that it's a test. I let them read it any way they want. Some chose to read it to themselves silently, some chose to read it with a group.

Pat: Did you have to read it to any of them?

Barb: No, because they were reading it together as a group. The only thing I'm going to have to do now is read the questions aloud for some of them. It's too difficult for some of them to read and when they gave us the tests for first graders, they let us read the questions. They have to answer it on their own. But I let them know what the question says.

Pat: Were there any specific instructions?

Barb: No. Because on the first grade test it'll ask a question and then it'll say circle an answer and there's three answers. It's a multiple choice. We've just done the first page and there were three questions and so I read the questions to them. And I read the three multiple choice and they picked them.

Laura: Were they in a group at that time?

Barb: They were in a group; but they all had folders covering their papers.

Margaret: So they're doing the actual test by themselves.

Karen: How often did they have to read the story? Did you tell them about the story?

Barb: I'm trying to think. It didn't take them very long. The older ones took a little longer, and the first graders didn't take as long. I would say not more than seven minutes, because they read it as a total group. [*Karen:*

Oh, so just all in one sitting, then.] Uh-huh. [*Karen:* They didn't go back and read it a second time or something like that.] No, because they can do that as we go along. The instructions at the top say, "Keep your book with you because if you want to look up an answer, you can."

Karen: So we need to plan out with those second graders.

Barb: Now, see, it took them longer because some groups finished quicker. I would say half an hour it took some of them to read it.

Karen: I need to borrow your copy sometime.

Barb: Right, so I'll be finished early with them. We only have one set of second grade books, don't we?

Margaret: I have several third graders who can't read it.

Barb: Well, my groups are reading aloud.

Margaret: Just pair them with somebody and they always pick someone who they know will support them.

Barb: Those that choose to are reading aloud. And so did those that wanted to know what the story says and to be able to discuss it. They can read well enough to follow along and everything.

This discussion shows teachers using each other as a resource and asking clarifying questions. They all had to deal with the tests and wanted to find an approach that didn't contradict the ways in which their students interacted with literature on a regular basis in their classrooms. While the discussion on testing was not about the main topic of field notes, the facilitator did not step in because it was clear that the topic was of immediate importance and offered a high level of engagement for the teachers. Kathy assumed that the group would return to the main focus once they had clarification from Barb.

Laura: What do you do with your incredible behavior problems that won't sit still? I mean do you stand up and say, "Pick a partner, I mean?" How did you do this?

Rena: I looked at their ability to read. I said, "OK, these are the ones that need the help and these are the ones that know how to read." And the ones that know how to read are the ones that did the picking. I said, "Who do you want of the people in the front. Pick one." Maybe that's not a good way to do it, but it sure did work when it came down to getting the assignment done. They were successful.

Barb: Yesterday, I had two boys who were going to go off alone and they were kind of behavior problems, so I said, "You need to work with a bigger group. I want more in a group today."

Rena: So you have to put a little bit of your judgement into it but you give a choice.

Barb: It depends on what you're going to do.

Margaret: The kids have learned by this time. I have a few that don't read, but they're popular and they're not stupid. They know that they need a partner who can read and they pick somebody who can and so far it's worked out really well.

Karen: I think the issue, though, is that of capability itself. I say, "You have the first choice and if you don't make a good choice, then the choice is mine."

Margaret: Oh, sure. If they're just goofing around.

Karen: And that's very simple. We talk about "Are you making a choice of somebody you know you can work *well* with?"

Barb: That's true. Sometimes the choice is their's in my room and sometimes it's mine.

This was an interesting discussion because the other teachers in the group were upset that Rena would so openly label children. However, they didn't attack her practice but shared their own experiences to offer her other options.

Pat: Margaret, are you saying they don't read or they don't read at that grade level for the test?

Margaret: They have to read in a third grade book. There's no way that a few of those kids would be able to do that, but they are reading. I have one nonreader.

Karen: When Jose comes to read for my class with his buddy reader, he has all of the behaviors of a reader.

Margaret: Oh, yeah. And he is starting to read some. He really is, but there's no way he could pick up that third grade book for the test and read it so he'll have to sit with someone and he'll pick someone. They're all very willing and *eager* to be with him. You know, that's wonderful.

Barb: I don't know whether it has to do with multi-age classes or not, but I notice there's a lot of self-confidence with the readers, whether they're doing well or not. Anna had Beronica, who is a first grader, help her with her reading. I mean she could not do it and she went and got this first grader and said, "I want you to help me do this." They don't seem to find anything wrong with the mixture of skills back and forth.

Myna: I wish there were a way to let parents know how well kids are handling these issues.

Pat: Within the social realm too because Aaron in my room spends the morning in kindergarten and he asked a second grader to work with him. Not only did they want to play with him, but they wanted to work with him. And I don't know if that was because they come across as the teacher but it's a neat thing because he's not doing much as far as reading and writing.

Karen: I'm fascinated that certain kids always pick out somebody who's a much more capable reader or writer. I've got a few kids who work really well with somebody else who's almost equal to their level and the two of them sit and struggle together and it's this mutual support. And that's some of the most powerful learning where both kids are learning as much as the other. It's that kind of sharing but I think a lot of it has to do with that choice of not being *assigned* to that person permanently or assigned to this group or assigned to that group; but all of that choice is involved. It's very exciting to see.

Margaret: I had a cute experience yesterday. It was my first chance to take field notes because we haven't had literature groups for a while because of the opera. I sat down with this group and that little Senny is so funny. The minute I sat down, it's "Oh, she's writing." So she started taking over the group and then she turned and she said, "Ain't I good?" [Laughter] I said, "You're telling me." I wrote it down and just cackled. And then she started just directing them "Now what do you think, Ashley? Now what do you think? What do you think?" And you [to Kathy] said Nichole was doing that in the group you listened to.

Kathy: I think it was because I was taking field notes.

Margaret: Yeah. Now the first day I saw a lot more of that than I did today. Today they were used to my taking notes again and they just sat back and started talking about the book. They didn't seem to mind that I was there.

Karen: Have you found that it's different with literature?

Margaret: Than what?

Karen: That the kids who emerge as leaders in the literature discussion groups aren't necessarily the class leaders?

Margaret: Yeah. Definitely. You know, I've never seen Senny actually lead a group. Last week she saw that I got a big kick out of that.

Kathy: I'd like to go back to field notes and just see what other kinds of issues you have. One of my questions is "What did you learn by taking field notes? Was it something that was worthwhile for you?"

Over time, the group had learned to ask clarification questions when someone said something that bothered them. At first, members often made statements that passed quick judgement on another person without finding out what was meant by a particular statement. As a first-grade teacher, Pat was concerned when Margaret said her students couldn't read. Her question allowed Margaret the opportunity to explain. It is also interesting that the principal, Myna, participated in the group as a member and gained insight into what happens in classrooms.

While this conversation is again a sidetrack, Margaret brought the group back to the main focus. This movement back and forth and around the main focus was a characteristic of our dialogue. As occurred here, someone usually brought the conversation back to the main focus once the immediate concern was dealt with. Kathy, as facilitator, supported Margaret in the movement back to field notes when another group member made observations that went in yet another direction, because the rest of the group seemed ready to return to the field note focus. She knew the group would ignore her if they were not ready to return to the focus.

Sharon: I had to think more about what I was doing. I had to take a lot of things out of my mind and keep my mouth shut. I couldn't do all those things at once because I wasn't good enough at field notes to do that. I could only do one thing. There's a whole big difference in how I was taking notes earlier and how it was in the end because it went over a two-week time. So, in the beginning the notes are not as big as they are now because I had to tell myself "You can't do this" and "You can't do that" and "You've just got to focus on this" and it's really hard. I think we're so used to thinking "What am I going to say to get them to do this?" or all that stuff that's going on in your head. And all that stuff can't go on in my head and I do field notes at the same time. I have to think about it again after you've shown me what you did today to see if I can do it shorter. I needed to know what you left out. What you thought was important to write down and what you didn't write down. [Note: Sharon had asked Kathy to come to her classroom that day and to take field notes of a literature group discussion.]

Margaret: What did she leave out?

Sharon: She left out a lot. Like, I would write the whole sentence or conversation. She only wrote down the idea of what was happening. And I have to be able to translate that in my mind without all of those words. So that will be helpful to me in the shorter version.

Pat: I think field notes really make you aware of the level of the kids' thinking. Especially when you go back and you reread it and you can focus in on when they shift gears. And when they stopped sharing and when they stopped retelling and when they started getting into the real meat of the issue. I like it because it tells you the thinking across other areas and how they are relating to other things that have happened and other books and other incidents and how it plays into their lives. So it really helps you see—Are we indeed creating thinkers? Are we getting them to think? And analyze? And evaluate? And I think that's what we want to do. And then I was checking whether a child was doing this kind of thinking, like Kathleen did.

Kathy: Yeah, this is another level. I mean it's one more level of analysis off of the field notes.

Karen: After becoming more proficient at it, I think that could then help us with our planning in terms of when we go back to a whole group discussion.

Kathy: Yeah. Kathleen just eliminated projects for the next round of books because she realized that projects had taken over the discussion. And she told the kids that they were going to talk about what they thought of the book. So it changed how she structured the groups and what she was emphasizing in the groups.

Pat: It also changes what they're writing in their literature logs when kids go back and really look at what they're saying.

Kathy: Do you mean when you use the logs as a reflection?

Pat: Yeah. The literature log helps them reflect on whether they're just re-telling it or are they thinking. It also helps us know what they are thinking.

While Kathy's earlier remarks about Kathleen's use of field notes had not brought a response, Pat returned to these comments as the group moved back to discussing field notes. This looping back to earlier comments occurred frequently and was a natural characteristic of our dialogue. We couldn't assume that issues weren't important if they were not immediately discussed.

Laura: I have a lot of trouble with that. My students don't want to—they don't want to be *bothered* to write down their ideas. They would write nothing if that was ok. [*Pat:* Do you respond to their logs in writing?] Other than two or three, the majority of them really don't want to have to go to that trouble.

Margaret: Maybe they've just had too much at this point.

Laura: They're very negative. Well, that's why I always do the reading experiences for a while and then focus more on writing which includes reading. I never totally separate them; but the emphasis is more on one or the other. When we're doing a big literature discussion, they use those in combination.

Barb: Do you do authors' chairs often?

Laura: In which way? That phrase has been used in five different ways I can think of. How?

Barb: Well, in my classroom, we only use it when the children are writing their own stories, and they'll go up and share their story with the children. The reason I brought it up is because I've noticed that when my most immature writers discovered I did that, they started writing. They didn't want to be bothered with writing and just wanted to draw pictures but when they found out they could share in front of the class, they wanted to write something so they could share. So maybe if you shared some of the good literature logs . . .

Laura: You have to pull to get them to share. They don't care to share.

Manuel: Is that typical of that age group?

Laura: I don't know. It wasn't last year. It's typical of this group.

Pat: We've had those kids and I know it's not typical.

Margaret: Well, there's kids in there that put things down. You've got big powerful leaders that put that kind of stuff down. If Matt could have his way, we wouldn't ever read because he doesn't want to read. And so he tries to put it down. And especially last year when he had Luis and Derrick, see they'd all put it down and then the whole class has that bad attitude. It's really hard when you've got very powerful leaders. When you've got those leaders because the peer pressure is so strong.

Pat: We used to thrive on sharing.

Tom: Yeah, but if you get negative leaders doing those kinds of things . . .

Karen: That group thrives on sharing their own agenda. They want to talk about the stories I'm reading to them.

Laura: No, they want to talk about the basketball game last night while you're reading a story to them. They only want to talk about what *they* want to talk about but their agenda doesn't have anything to do with anything they're doing in the class if they're given a choice. Nothing. They do not want to discuss anything that you provide. It's very difficult and I've plowed through it all year long.

Barb: Maybe that's a key then. Maybe you should listen and see if you can go with some of those avenues that would be their agenda. For instance, do something really exciting with basketball. They've got all those cards and all that reading on the back of those cards. One at a time they'll buy these little plastic folders—and they come in with notebooks of them. Think up some things with these boys to do with those types of things.

Pat: Sharon has all the pictures of the players from the newspapers. Her kids have been bringing in all this basketball stuff. They're writing questions to the basketball players.

Karen: Have you seen any of the books by Matt Christopher?

Laura: Who's that?

Karen: He is a children's author who writes sports books about kids involved in sports, and they are at a reading level that's real appropriate for some of your kids.

Laura: That's the next thing I was about to say is I see very little that these kids have handled readingwise.

Karen: The Matt Christopher books have sports characters including girls in sports.

Sharon: But you can also use the newspaper. I don't have any basketball books for first graders. There will probably be some for your level; but there wouldn't be any for me. So I just use the newspapers.

Barb: Maybe you could get children to redo articles. Maybe they could cut out the picture and type on the computers in computer lab to make a new headline and summarize it in their own words. And make posters for around the school.

Pat: We had to go with the Ninja turtles for a while.

Karen: But this group really doesn't understand that negotiation sometimes means you don't get exactly what you want. That there's a time to be cooperative with the teacher and a time to follow your own interests. And I think there's a balance, and that's the issue I had to deal with last year with those kids. "It's my turn now. You have your turn. I have my turn."

Margaret: Yeah, same with spelling. They vote on their spelling words and I tried to sneak some words through one time and they didn't learn them. No way. They wouldn't do them. I threw the whole thing out and we went back to "Vote on your words." The ownership is real important.

Barb: Would you like more suggestions along that line? If some of us could think of ideas?

Laura: Yeah, that would be helpful. I hate the idea of doing sports because I dislike sports *so* intensely.

Karen: Well, then there's your challenge. That can be your challenge to the kids. "I really don't like sports. What I want you to do is persuade me."

Laura: That's a good idea.

Margaret: Yeah, you'll go along with their interest level for a while, then it's negotiable and you can bring in some ideas too.

Laura: I like that, that's an interesting idea.

———————

At several points during this session, Laura had asked questions that seemed to indicate frustration with her class. Here her issues took over the discussion. Several group members initially challenged her statements, but when they realized her deep frustration and her need for their support as colleagues, the tone shifted. Others acknowledged problems with that particular group of students and provided empathetic support. They also brainstormed suggestions, carefully checking to make sure that this is what she wanted. Throughout this discussion, Laura took a lot of risks. She was honest about her feelings and the problems. She didn't blame other teachers and was confident enough in her own teaching to know that this was an unusual situation where she desperately needed their ideas. This situation is a good example of the group's willingness to abandon the agenda to deal with a personal issue of one teacher.

Barb: I have a question. If you have any information on the Cheyenne or quilling, could you let me know?

Kathy: I have a question too. We have just two study group times left this year. The last meeting will primarily be reflection. What do we want to do at our next meeting?

Margaret: Could we keep doing these field notes? Maybe some people don't need this, but I need to go further than "What do you do with them?"

Kathy: You mean what I was describing with analyzing them?

Margaret: Yeah, that kind of analysis stuff.

Kathy: To actually do the analysis here?

Margaret: I don't know. Maybe some time looking at them in small groups.

Pat: If you spend time really looking at them, it kind of pops out at you.

Sharon: Maybe take one person's notes.

Leslie: I want to know how to do analysis. I don't want to stop with field notes.

Kathy: My other question is we spent so much time in the fall on portfolios, and I don't want to force the group to go back to it; but is there anything we need to tie up with that?

Margaret: No, because we've been mandated by the district on what we have to do. We don't have any choice. It's like they zapped us and we don't have a choice.

Sharon: But we can put in the things they didn't talk about.

Laura: It's on the last page in small print that you can also include other things. It was on the third or fourth page in small print at the top of one little page that you could also include these things.

Kathy: When is that due?

Laura: The end of the year. We've got to turn those in. Those have to go with the kids. They become a section of the "cum" folder. Part of it replaces some other existing forms we had and then it also adds enormously to them.

Karen: But those kids who are older have all that other stuff in there.

Laura: It isn't supposed to consolidate. It's suppose to regulate! It's going to regiment. They want an exact form and everybody's going to use the same form in the same way!

Barb: Well, but the whole thing is if all teachers in the district would be doing something, then the district wouldn't force us to do this.

Laura: That's right. That's exactly right. And they're making sure that those that don't do their part *will* do their part because they'll make them.

Margaret: Also they want something that you can send from school to home.

Kathy: Any other ideas for what to discuss next time?

Several voices: Let's continue with field notes.

Kathy: So for next time, we will continue to focus on field notes and spend some time sharing our notes and then analyzing them. Is that what you were suggesting? Or does someone have a different idea for how we should proceed?

Several voices: Sounds good.

———————

Barb's question and the time on the clock indicated that the group needed to move into negotiating the agenda for the next meeting. There was fairly quick consensus on what to discuss next because it was clear that we were in the middle of our discussion about field notes and wanted to continue.

Kathy's question about portfolios brought out strong feelings of frustration over an issue the group had earlier discussed—their sense that district administrators constantly created new mandates that were meant to force "weak" teachers to teach in particular ways. The problem was that the mandates aimed too low because they focused on "weak" teachers and restricted what others were attempting in their classrooms. The group had earlier explored student-created portfolios that involved a complex process of student selection and reflection on ongoing work. When the district mandated a portfolio that was teacher-directed with collections of required writing samples and checklists, many teachers angrily abandoned their efforts. That anger is evident in their remarks at the end of our meeting. The group felt strongly that instead of mandates being directed at correcting "weak" teaching, the district should encourage the practices of effective, innovative teachers while providing additional help for those needing more support in their teaching.

———————

The meeting ended as usual with many different conversations occurring at once. Most continued talking as they left the library to return to their classrooms, while a few lingered in the library to discuss the issues raised in the session. A week later, the following notes were distributed:

Warren Study Group Notes
April 9

Sharing: Children's responses to books such as *Twenty & Ten*

Focus: Field notes as a form of evaluation

- Ways of quickly taking notes: use children's initials, put names at top of paper; get key phrases, ideas, gist; not everything said; don't write in complete sentences
- Advantages and disadvantages of using tape recorder: listen to the tape on the way home from school; signals that this discussion is important
- Notes help teachers know what is happening in group and get a sense of the level of student thinking
- Can use notes to refocus a group, summarize the discussion for the students, take discussion to a deeper level
- Taking notes cuts down on teacher-domination of talk
- Can analyze the notes, using categories
- Can share notes/transcripts with students

Also discussed:

- Students reflecting on what they are discussing in literature circles and how groups are functioning
- Ways to use literature circles as part of testing
- Children choosing whom they will read with
- Motivating resistant readers

Next meeting: April 30. Bring field notes and we will analyze the notes to find categories to describe what is happening in the literature discussions.

Conclusion

We debated for a long time whether or not to write this chapter and include a transcript. We finally decided to do so because we wanted to show the reality of the interactions and discussions in the study group. Even though we had agreed on a focus for the session, getting off track on other related issues was a natural part of our dialogue. We shared the connections and issues that the conversations were raising in our minds. We weren't restricted to a particular person's topic or agenda. We knew that we could explore related issues and then come back to our main topic. The study group was focused, but not tightly regulated or structured.

Another reason for including this transcript was to demonstrate the range of voices in our discussions. These voices reflected different theoretical perspectives and viewpoints about teaching. Study group sessions allowed us to hear many of our colleagues and to contemplate a variety of perspectives.

Finally, it was through the analysis of many transcripts such as this one that we were able to gain insights into the study group process. We spent many hours analyzing the talk and interactions in order to gain a better understanding of the dynamics of the group, the role of the facilitator, and the factors that influenced whether or not a session was productive. While we did this analysis for research purposes, it quickly became apparent that the analysis was essential to the continuation of the groups. The importance of reflection and analysis to the study group is discussed further in Chapter 7.

As we analyzed transcripts such as the one included in this chapter, we identified the major kinds of talk in which the facilitator and group members engaged. The following summarizes these major categories and may be helpful as you think about your own group and the kinds of talk which are or are not occurring:

 Facilitator Talk

Sharing

A facilitator . . .

- Shares ideas for group consideration or as part of the group discussion. Sharing implies that these ideas are offered as suggestions, something for others to consider, rather than presented in a formal way as "truth." Instead of holding others at a distance, sharing invites collaboration and the willingness to take in others' points of view.

- Shares references to professional literature, children's literature, and classroom experiences as well as own learning experiences as an educator, personal struggles, and beliefs.

Supporting

A facilitator . . .

- Supports and encourages individuals in their own growth through non-judgmental comments that are replies to, rather than judgments of, comments made by participants. Supporting also involves encouraging others to take the risk to share their thoughts, feelings, and ideas, both professionally and personally.
- Makes connections between the study group and individual classrooms by sharing what the facilitator has seen in others' classrooms or by encouraging others to share.
- Provides protection so that group members feel free to share their beliefs and practices without being attacked.

Questioning

A facilitator . . .

- Asks questions or makes comments that encourage participants to challenge their beliefs, each other, or the educational system.
- Encourages participants to consider particular issues in greater depth or from a different perspective. Questions take the form of replies that signal that the other person's point of view has been taken seriously, even though others may want to extend or modify what the person has said. Replying stands in contrast to assessment, which measures what someone has said against an external standard.

Building Community

A facilitator . . .

- Makes comments or asks questions to encourage interaction among group members and to distribute talk among more members.
- Maintains discussion by remembering questions posed by group members and referring back to those questions.
- Facilitates discussion of issues where individuals have different perspectives or are at different points in their own professional growth. Instead of directing the discussion to one particular point, the facilitator encourages the discussion of a variety of points on that issue.
- Must also be aware of the conflict and undercurrents present in the school that may be having an impact on the group discus-

sion and the willingness of certain individuals to interact in the group.

Negotiating

A facilitator . . .

- Works to collaboratively set structures and agendas.
- Negotiates decisions about the group agenda, readings, structure of sessions with group members.

Clarifying/Summarizing

A facilitator . . .

- Asks questions to encourage group members to clarify the beliefs or ideas they are sharing.
- Makes statements that summarize points of discussion.

Humor

A facilitator . . .

- Laughs or jokes with the group.

 ## Talk of Group Members

Sharing

Group members . . .

- Share personal experiences and beliefs based on practice, theory, and research as suggestions to be considered by the group. These beliefs and practices come from actual experience in the classroom, conversations with or presentations by other educators, and professional readings.
- May also share examples from life experiences outside of school or serve as a resource for specific information from district committees or professional references.
- Share their ideas as part of the group process, rather than presenting ideas or information as "truths." The use of presentational language, such as "you should" or "you need," implies that "I know something and you need to know it."
- Share options that others might consider instead of telling other teachers what they need to do. Taking on the voice of an expert who tells others what to do closes down discussion.

Risk-Taking

Group members . . .

- Share "rough draft" ideas or beliefs that they are thinking through for themselves. They might share something new they are trying in their classrooms and aren't quite sure about but are willing to give a try.
- Take risks and openly share questions or struggles they are having with the whole group.
- Challenge their beliefs and openly admit they don't really know something. They are willing to share with the group even though they do not know how others will "hear" what they are saying.

Supporting/Listening

Group members . . .

- Actively support others in the group by encouraging them to share about their classroom or by making comments that are supportive of others' efforts at working through practice and beliefs.
- Support each other by assuming a listening stance and making empathetic statements that signal they are trying to understand another group member. Responses to others are replies, not judgments.

Questioning

Group members . . .

- Ask each other questions to clarify, raise new issues, or challenge others to consider a different perspective on their practice or beliefs. Sometimes the challenges are professional challenges or replies where teachers are working together to extend their thinking in positive ways. When the challenge is a negative personal attack or judgement on another person's teaching, this shuts down discussion.

Clarifying/Summarizing

Group members . . .

- Clarify points of confusion.
- Summarize comments by others.

Suggesting

Group members . . .

- Offer each other suggestions on issues related to theory and practice or on how the study group might operate.

Reflecting

Group members . . .

- Reflect on the meanings of practice and beliefs by moving from sharing an experience to reflecting on the beliefs/theories underlying that experience.
- Discuss changes in their thinking and raise new questions because of experiences, especially an "Ah ha!" experience.

Expressing Disequilibrium

Group members . . .

- Talk about questions or concerns they have and about which they are feeling some turmoil and uncertainty.
- Express fears, vent frustrations, and voice despair and major tension.

Humor

Group members . . .

- Use humor to respond to each other.

6 What Are the Issues that Study Groups Confront?

In many ways, creating a study group as a context for dialogue seems simple and straightforward. It makes sense that educators need places where they talk their way into understandings with each other and form networks that support their thinking and work in schools. However, given the dependence of study groups on collaborative relationships and exploratory talk and their existence within hierarchial school structures, it's not surprising that study groups often face difficult times. In this chapter, we highlight the major problems that we encountered.

We raise these issues not to discourage others from starting a study group, but to give a sense of the struggles that you might face. We also hope that you might be able to avoid some of the mistakes that we've made. We share these with the firm belief that despite the struggles that seem to be an inherent part of study groups, these groups play a valued and critical role in our lives as educators. They are worth the struggle. Their messiness is part of our complexity as human beings.

Should Study Groups Be Used to Mandate Change?

One way to ensure the failure of a study group is to mandate attendance or to establish the group as a place where participants feel forced to change their teaching. Collaborative relationships grow out of the willingness of all participants to engage in dialogue with others. Mandated attendance works against these relationships and creates resistance and may lead some to undermine the group. For the same reasons, participants resent the group if they feel that they are judged as "deficient" and that others are trying to "fix" their teaching. They respond defensively and feel unsafe in the group.

Study groups often do address issues related to curricular mandates within the school district, but these mandates are ones that teachers *want* to talk about with their colleagues. This decision needs to be made by teachers, not someone higher up in the system. Productive dialogue will not occur when teachers are discussing issues that are not of major significance to them.

This dialogue will also not occur if the group is being used by others to force changes in teachers' actions. The group is no longer a safe place for risk-taking. Requiring that change occur for all teachers at the same time does not recognize the different ways in which teachers learn—some constantly make changes in their practices and then watch to see what happens, while others think through issues for a long period of time before taking action in their classrooms. Taking new action is a natural outcome of the group but it is encouraged, not mandated. We also want to reiterate that for us change is inherent to professional growth, not something that is forced upon us because something is wrong with our teaching.

What about New Members?

One of the issues we struggled with during our second year was the changing dynamics brought about by new teachers joining the group. Several were new to the building and several were long-time staff members who joined for the first time. While we were excited by the growth and glad to have these colleagues, the new situation also created some difficulties.

First, there was the need to reestablish a sense of community, trust, and safety for our discussions. The addition of new members affected these dynamics, and it took some time for everyone to feel safe again. Secondly, the new members sometimes brought up issues for the agenda that had been discussed in depth the previous year. The returning members didn't want to rehash those discussions, but felt guilty at saying "We don't want to talk about this" when it was a critical issue for others. For example, the Maldonado group spent several months talking about portfolios only to have several new members the following year again propose portfolios. The returning members groaned at the thought, while the new members looked puzzled and a bit offended that their proposal was received negatively.

We never found the perfect solution to this dilemma. Sometimes the group agrees to return to the topic, but from a slightly different perspective. For example, the Maldonado group revisited portfolios but looked at reflection and self-evaluation portfolios that were child-generated instead of portfolios used by teachers for their evaluation. Other times, the group suggests other ways the individual could deal with the issue. For example, a new teacher suggested that the Warren group bring their schedules to share. The group had done this the previous year and didn't want to repeat this experience. Members explained the problem and one volunteered to meet with the teacher to talk about schedules outside the group.

When Does a Study Group Need Outside Experts?

An issue that we revisited a number of times was the role of outside experts in the study group. We see ourselves as experts who create knowledge through our talk together but we also value the ideas of outside experts and include their ideas in several ways. One is through professional readings where we identify an article, chapter, or book that provides perspective on an issue.

Occasionally the group makes a decision to invite an outside person to the group because of issues that are being raised. For example, after we had discussed portfolios for several months and reached some common understandings, we invited a central administrator to our next meeting so that we could learn more about the district's plan for portfolios. We began that meeting by sharing what we had discussed about portfolios, and several teachers talked about what they were doing in their classrooms. We then asked the administrator to talk about the district's efforts. We carefully set up the meeting so that the administrator wasn't presenting to us, and thus we defined the agenda. We spent the next study group meeting talking about our response to this session.

The study group at Fort Lowell invited Kathy to one of their meetings as an outside expert on inquiry-based curriculum. They were discussing an integrated thematic approach that their school was thinking of adopting and had many questions about how this approach related to inquiry. They had read various articles and had participated in many discussions among themselves. When they decided to invite Kathy, they first brainstormed a list of questions and issues that they gave to her ahead of time. The study group session was not a presentation by Kathy, but an interactive discussion on the issues, in which Kathy participated.

From these experiences, we decided that the best way to handle a guest is to spend the session preceding the visit thinking through what *we* want to talk about with our guest and to send the guest these issues and questions ahead of time. We begin these sessions with group members talking about their concerns about the issues as related to the focus and invite the guest to become part of our conversation. Often we spend the following study group session reflecting on our conversation with the guest.

Can Principals Be Contributing Members of the Group?

Principals can play a valued and valuable role in the group process; however, the principal's presence can also destroy a sense of safety so that teachers are unwilling to openly share their thinking and explorations. The decision about principal membership needs to be made carefully by the group. While we believe principals should be members, we know that each group will need to consider this issue and make their own decision.

In the Warren and Maldonado study groups, the principals participated in discussions, offering suggestions and sharing their thinking as part of the group process. One of the positive benefits of having the principal present in the group was the opportunity to talk as equals about teaching. The principal came as a teacher, not as the administrator or evaluator. Instead of conducting business or taking care of a school crisis, the principal could pull back from "administrivia" and think about curriculum and teaching with other educators. This opportunity was valued by everyone involved. It established a sense of knowing each other, personally and professionally, that influenced relationships across the school day and year. It led to an appreciation of each other as colleagues. Teachers and principals became more aware of how the other thought about educational issues and this awareness, in turn, influenced relationships outside the group.

Another benefit was that the principal's presence legitimized the group for some teachers. The fact that the principal took time to come, listen, and participate signaled that the study group was valued as part of the school structure.

In reflecting on her membership in the study group, Myna Matlin, principal at Warren, noted that she found herself thinking differently about teachers outside of the study group. "I realized that teachers really are thoroughly thinking through what they are doing in the classroom much more than I had previously thought. When something bombs, I hear people in the group and at lunch talking about it now. It was not a poorly developed lesson." She went on to say, "I see situations where in the past I would have said, 'I wish this was different' about something in someone's classroom without understanding the *why* behind what was going on. Now I see what is being attempted and try to make suggestions because of the study group discussions. The group gives me a chance to see into people's thinking. I might not agree with opinions or approaches but I have gained added respect for everyone in some way."

Both Myna Matlin and Virginia Romero, principal at Maldonado, found that they were much more aware of what needed to be dealt with at the school level. This awareness led to changes in agendas for staff meetings and school inservices. As Virginia noted, "I see what's important to teachers. The group is a sounding board for different directions

I am thinking about. I know they will respond honestly to my ideas." It also led Myna to change how she spent her time. "I realized I need to be in classrooms more so I can keep up with and be more of a support for teachers and so I can see what kids are doing."

Although the role of the principal within the group was to listen and participate as an equal, teachers were quite aware that the discussions influenced the principal's evaluation of them outside the group. Principals have a great deal of power within schools, and some teachers felt uncomfortable talking about their fears and mistakes in the principal's presence. Although they trusted the principal not to directly use the information against them, they feared that talking about their problems would indirectly influence the principal's view of them as effective teachers.

Even when teachers trusted and respected their principal, the principal's presence did initially have a negative influence on teachers' willingness to share about difficult issues. Most teachers carefully monitored the principal's participation in the first sessions. If the principal dominated discussions or moved into "administrator talk," some chose not to talk or dropped out of the group. If the principal listened, offered occasional comments, and shared doubts and fears, most teachers were able to accept and value the principal as a member. There were several teachers in each group, however, who never felt completely comfortable with the principal's presence even after three years. Sometimes this was because of previous negative experiences with other principals and other times was due to their own strained relationship with the current principal.

A related issue was that whenever a principal introduced a possible agenda focus, teachers often felt obligated to take on that issue. The facilitator can play a critical role at this point by acknowledging the principal's suggestion and asking for additional issues so that multiple suggestions are available to the group. Principals and administrators need to recognize that their position gives them power and that they need to offer suggestions in a tentative manner without pushing their ideas.

In one case, a principal began to use the group to solve problems she was facing in the school. While it is appropriate to raise these problems during sharing, the principal's problems started taking over the group focus. We worked as facilitators to make sure that the group stayed with their focus and the principal's agenda didn't dominate the group on a regular basis.

At the end of the first year of our study group, the summer research group had extensive conversations about whether or not the principal should be a member of the study group. Based on the interviews, it was clear that teachers valued the principal's presence, but still felt constrained in what they were willing to share. We finally decided that while ideally the principal should be a member of the group, the decision of whether or not the principal is invited should be the teachers' decision. If a group feels uncomfortable or unsafe with the principal's presence to the point of not being willing to openly discuss issues, then they should seriously consider asking the principal not to join. It may be that once the group has become comfortable talking with each other the principal could then be invited. In some cases, the decision not to invite the principal may reflect more about teachers' personalities and their difficulty getting beyond traditional hierarchies than any real problem with the principal. In other cases, the issue may reflect serious problems in how a particular principal operates within the school.

In several study groups, the principal has made the decision not to join the group. In the Fort Lowell group, for example, the principal knew that teachers were feeling resentment over a number of curricular changes that she had introduced into the school. She realized that they needed an opportunity to voice that resentment and talk through these curriculum issues with each other. Because she had introduced the changes, the discussions would not occur if she were present. She did, however, indicate to the group that she was willing to come and answer questions or participate at whatever point they wanted her presence, and the group later took her up on her offer.

The purpose for the study group is to create a "zone of safety" (Lipka & McCarty, 1994) where educators can openly discuss their beliefs and practices and find support and challenge to their ways of operating within their teaching contexts. This purpose is the key factor to consider when making decisions about the membership of educators who are in positions of power over the members for whom the group was established. A teacher study group exists first and foremost as a place for teachers to safely examine the issues of teaching and curriculum. If the presence of the principal has a major negative impact on the group's willingness to talk, then the principal should not be a member of the group.

What about Parents as Members of a Study Group?

Another related issue is the presence of parents and community members in study groups. Some study groups are established as a place for community members and educators to meet and talk together about educational issues. These groups provide a powerful context for understanding each other's perspectives and learning to think and work together. At Ochoa Elementary School, for example, a community coalition group was formed that seeks solutions to local problems and ways to bring community issues into the school curriculum (Heckman, 1996).

However, it is not always appropriate for parents to be included. Kathy worked with a teacher study group where teachers were exploring new curricular ideas related to inquiry. They had many concerns and questions as they tried new approaches in their classrooms and were reluctant to talk about these issues in front of parents. They needed the study group to function as a zone of safety where they could talk about their struggles. They needed to explore ideas that were on the "edge" of their current understandings—ideas that they couldn't yet discuss with fluency or coherency. When the principal invited parents from the school parent council to join the study group, discussions immediately closed down. A compromise was reached where parents were invited to certain sessions. In those sessions, the discussion was on shared issues such as standardized testing or the school discipline policy or curricular issues with which teachers felt more comfortable, such as using literature rather than a basal.

While the purpose of a study group is to explore issues of mutual interest, the success of a study group depends upon trust. Unless all members are taking the same risks, trust will be hard to establish. It is not always possible for a person outside of the profession to understand the growth dynamics inherent in a line of work. And if these misunderstandings are shared outside the context of the group, it could lead to a rift between the school and community. Confidentiality is essential.

From this experience it was clear that parents who become members of a study group need to come as participants to explore issues and not as evaluators to tell teachers what is wrong. The study group is a place for everyone to think, explore, and ask questions about topics of common concern. Identifying productive issues that concern all participants is essential. For example, study groups of teachers, parents, and community members have been very effective in thinking through broad-based goals for the school or dealing with community problems that affect children or the school.

Ideally, study groups are open and inclusive—whoever wants to join the group should be able to do so. The broader the membership, the greater the diversity of perspectives and this diversity challenges all group members to think in new ways. The reality, however, is that people must feel safe to put their "rough draft" thinking out for consideration. For dialogue to occur, participants must be willing to be vulnerable and to question their own theories and practices. The benefits of inclusive membership must always be weighed against creating this zone of safety for curriculum reform and professional growth.

What about Commitment, Continuity, and Confidentiality?

The issue of membership brings up the problem of sporadic attendance and people dropping in and out of the group. The reality is that typically only one-half to two-thirds of the group is present at any given meeting and different people are absent each time. This fluctuation can destroy continuity, making it impossible for the group to continue previous discussions—essentially the group starts over at each meeting. This lack of continuity is very discouraging to those who attend every meeting, and it can result in their feeling that they are not benefiting from the group.

We tried a number of strategies to encourage regular attendance. One was to discuss the norms of the group at the first meeting and to establish commitment as one of the norms. Another was to encourage everyone to participate in the discussions and in the decision making. The facilitator played a key role in inviting comments from those who weren't participating. People who didn't feel they had a voice were much more likely to be sporadic in attendance. In addition, putting notes from each meeting into everyone's mail-slots indicating the date and focus for the next meeting was a constant invitation for new members and a reminder to continuing members.

We also found that once or twice a year we needed to spend a session reflecting on the quality of our meetings and to openly discuss ways to improve that quality. In general, if we were sensitive to the needs and concerns of members when planning logistics and agenda, members were more committed to the group. Specific and relevant tasks between meetings tended to increase interest and responsibility as long as these were not too time consuming. Also, if we rotated various roles such as facilitator and notetaker among group members, they became fuller participants in the study group process. Finally, getting the study group approved for district increment credit provided an additional incentive for attendance.

A related issue is that of coming prepared for the session when the group has agreed to read an article or to engage in an activity in their classrooms. A few people coming unprepared does not create major problems, but sometimes only a few are prepared and they resent that no one else has followed through. We found in that case that we needed to have a frank discussion as a group about what to do. In some cases, the group decided they were just too busy or too stressed to do anything between meetings. In other cases, the group decided that they did want to read or engage in certain activities but just needed to reduce the amount. This discussion created a stronger sense of shared responsibility among members.

This issue needs to be handled carefully because some members dropped out of our groups. They felt they didn't have time to read between sessions and that therefore they couldn't come. We wanted members to feel responsible for being prepared, but we also felt that we would rather have someone come unprepared than leave the group.

We consider confidentiality as essential to the group and usually discuss it at the first meeting each year. If study groups are a zone of safety for struggling with ideas and beliefs that really matter to participants, then they must be able to trust others to maintain confidentiality. We also immediately raise the issue if someone has broken that confidentiality—not to point a finger at a particular person, but to reiterate that confidentiality is at the heart of the group.

Sometimes issues are raised in the group that need to be dealt with outside of the group. In those cases, members have asked permission to take these issues to a staff meeting or some other appropriate place. The individuals involved decide what can and cannot be shared outside the study group.

What about Food?

Food may seem insignificant in comparison to the other issues we are raising, but it can have a major influence on a meeting. Sharing refreshments often plays a key role in creating informal social environments which invite conversation and relationships. The Maldonado group always had snacks and spent time deciding who would bring what for the following meeting. Group members came to the meeting depleted of energy from a long day and they looked forward to the food and the conversation.

However, one problem was that these decisions took away valuable time from the group. A focus on snacks also sometimes made it difficult to start the meeting on time because everyone was moving around to get something to eat. In addition, refreshments can invite an atmosphere that is too informal, so that talk remains social and there are many side conversations.

The Warren study group usually did not have food at their meetings for these reasons. Teachers occasionally brought their own snacks or drinks. Later when the committee organized the study group sessions, they brought popcorn or some other type of snack which could be put in bowls at each table so members could immediately settle in at a table and begin the sharing time.

How Does the Group Deal with Conflict and Difficult Relationships?

One of the surprising side effects of the study group during the first year at Warren was that the amount of conflict in the school increased. Warren was a typical school in that conflict was something to be avoided. Teachers talked about each other behind the scenes and avoided people whom they disliked or disagreed with. Various cliques had formed within the school, and rarely did teachers associate with someone out of their own clique. The study group brought everyone together in a context where they needed to talk with each other about beliefs that were significant to them as teachers. Differences of opinion and personality clashes could no longer remain hidden. They came above ground—not always in the group itself, but often in the hallways after the meeting.

These same issues of conflict have emerged in other study groups as well. In one group, divisions among teachers that went back twenty years—when some went on strike and others did not—had to be discussed before the study group could proceed. In other groups, conflicts have reflected long-term racial, political, and theoretical divisions between teachers, power structures that are well embedded into the life of the school, and differences related to participation in particular programs, such as intermediate and primary, bilingual, and gifted programs.

We realized first of all that it was better for the conflict to come out in the open than to fester below the surface. We also had to recognize that conflict plays an essential role in our growth as educators and as people. If everyone agrees on everything, there's really nothing to discuss and no reason to meet. It's through conflict and difference that we are challenged to define our theory and articulate what we believe. In fact, we would argue that if there is no conflict in a group, something is wrong, either in relationships or in the choice of topic under discussion.

However, conflict can turn nasty and personal. We made clear distinctions between challenging someone's perspective and personally attacking that person. Facilitators played a key role in making this distinction, stepping in immediately to facilitate the talk if it became too personal or heated. If the conversation turned to personal conflicts, the facilitator often redirected the conversation back to broader professional issues. For example, in one discussion the intermediate teachers felt they were being attacked by the primary teachers on issues related to the conduct of their students in the hallways and in the cafeteria. The primary teachers believed that the rules weren't being followed and that particular intermediate teachers weren't doing their job. The intermediate teachers felt that the primary teachers didn't understand ten- and eleven-year old children and assumed they were the same as six-year-olds. When it became clear that the discussion was dissolving into teachers blaming teachers, the facilitator asked a broader question about teachers' beliefs about discipline and the need for consistency across teachers. This was a more productive discussion and teachers found common ground in some of their basic beliefs, even though there were differences in their practices.

In another case, a group discussed differences in their beliefs about whether or not children need to know mathematical facts. While everyone accepted the need for children to use mathematics as a way to think through problems and not just fill in math worksheets, some believed that children also needed some drill on facts while others did not. Complicating this discussion was a strong personal conflict between several of the teachers who took opposite sides on this issue. The group quickly dissolved into a strong clash in which no one listened to the other person, but rushed to quickly make the next point. When the facilitator was drawn into the heated debate, she directed the discussion back to broader issues about mathematics as a way of thinking and problem solving, in which calculations played a role but weren't the primary focus of attention. She asked whether it might be an issue of emphasis rather than elimination of approaches and pointed out that it appeared that some people seemed to be in agreement but were using different language.

We learned a lot from this experience and have used those understandings in other sessions where discussion became heated. One strategy the facilitator can use in this situation is to slow down the conversation so that members really listen to each other instead of immediately jumping in with their comments. Sometimes the facilitator restates what someone has said and then checks with that person, "Is this what you are saying?" The facilitator can also stop members from interrupting each other, asking them to hold their comments until that person has finished talking. Another strategy is to invite others to participate by asking if anyone else has a perspective on the particular issue.

It's also important to decide when a further discussion of the issue is no longer productive—the discussion is going around in circles with the same points being made. At that point, it's often helpful to say "Let's agree to disagree on this point" and ask the group what other issues they would like to discuss related to the focus of that meeting. Another possibility is to ask if anyone has professional reading that might be used for the next session to provide some clarity on the issue.

There may be some group members who assume that any challenge is a personal attack. For them, differences of opinion are always to be avoided. In a literature discussion of adult books from multicultural perspectives, several members challenged one person's interpretation of a novel. Their comments were not personal criticisms, but meant to offer another interpretation from the one he was proposing. However, he saw this difference of opinion as an attack and stopped coming to the group. He felt unsafe in a situation where members challenged each other's thinking as a way to push their understandings. Despite individuals going to him privately, he was unwilling to rejoin the group.

One of the most difficult issues we faced were strained personal relationships between group members. Sometimes these related to past histories and conflicts. Other times, there was a clash of personalities, values, or lifestyles of individuals who wouldn't normally choose to be in a group together. All of us have faced situations where we simply do not get along with another individual because of these differences.

Within the group, we had to clarify that the purpose of the group wasn't that everyone like each other on a personal level. That was an unrealistic and inappropriate goal for the group. It was our goal that we understand each other as professionals, whether we agreed or not. Within sessions, the facilitator needed to be aware of conflicts that were personal, rather than professional in nature and facilitate the talk accordingly.

One of the changes we noted over time was in relation to people's attitudes toward each other. In the end-of-the-year interviews, teachers talked about these changes. At the end of the first year, several talked about their personal dislike of particular individuals and how difficult it was to listen to that person in the group. By the end of the second year, those same teachers talked about being able to tolerate that person in the group. And by the end of the third year, they talked about gaining a sense of respect for those individuals even though they still disagreed professionally and had little social interaction with them. They had developed a professional relationship without feeling they also had to have a personal relationship with that person.

What about Group Members Who Dominate or Remain Silent?

Everyone has experienced being part of a discussion that is dominated by several individuals while others sit silently. Both responses are a concern within a study group. It is inevitable that some members will talk more than others and in many cases other members value the contributions of those individuals and encourage their talk. We don't see this as a problem unless their contributions keep others out of the conversation.

We never completely solved the issue of particular individuals dominating the discussion, but we did try several strategies. Our most common strategy was to step in as a facilitator to invite others to contribute. It was important to first acknowledge the dominator's contribution so that the person did not feel dismissed and then ask if anyone else had something to share about the issue under discussion. In one extreme case, one of us met with the teacher who was dominating the discussions and shared transcripts of study group sessions so she could see how her talk was negatively affecting the group. We wanted her to understand that she made valuable contributions to the group but was taking so much talk time that others were growing increasingly resentful of her presence.

The contrasting situation is group members who rarely or never talk. Inviting these members to share needs to be done carefully so they don't feel that attention is focused on them in an embarrassing way. Often, even if these individuals have something to say, they are unwilling to push their way into a discussion. The talk in some of our sessions was very intense, with comments flying quickly back and forth across the room. The most effective strategy was for the facilitator to watch for a brief space and to slow down the conversation by asking, "Is there anyone who hasn't had a chance to share who wants to say something?" By quickly making eye contact with those who have not been talking, a facilitator can encourage them to make a comment without embarrassing them by calling on them.

Kathy found that the discussions in the principal study group were often so intense that group members had to speak over one another in order to get their voices into the discussion. The person who spoke the loudest and didn't give up was able to get the floor. As a facilitator, Kathy carefully watched the group to see when the quieter individuals had something to say but were not successfully pushing their way into the conversation. In those cases, she pushed her way into the discussion and turned the floor over to those persons.

We also recognize that individuals should have the right to choose not to talk. Silence is not necessarily an indication that the person feels silenced. Some individuals listen thoughtfully and only occasionally make a short statement. When they do talk, others listen carefully out of respect for that person's thoughtfulness. In other cases, some people feel overwhelmed by the newness of the study group context and need time to listen to the conversations and figure out how they fit within the group.

Others wait until they feel a sense of community and trust before being willing to share.

A related issue is that some members take on the mantle of authority and make statements of fact that shut down discussion. They position themselves as experts who cannot be questioned, thereby silencing other participants. Douglas Barnes (1976) makes the distinction between sharing and presenting. Presentational talk involves presenting a view of self as you want others to see you, but without allowing them to see behind your carefully constructed facade. This type of talk often relies on statements of authority—"research says" or "everyone knows." In contrast, when participants engage in sharing, they abandon their facades and share personal experiences and beliefs. Sharing "implies collaboration and the willingness to take in the other's point of view, rather than holding it at arm's length" (p. 110). Barnes goes on to note that whenever we feel that others judge us and note our inadequacies, we are more likely to "put on a display" and focus on whether what we are saying is acceptable.

Barnes further distinguishes between replying and assessing. Replying consists of carefully listening to what someone says and building from that comment. To reply is to signal that the person has been taken seriously and to encourage the person to extend the conversation. In contrast, assessing involves judging someone's comment. There is no room for a difference of opinion or continued discussion because the person's comment has been measured against an external standard and found lacking. Replying talk is an invitation to continue a conversation while assessing shuts down the talk. In his research, Barnes found that when sharing and replying dominate a discussion, participants are encouraged to "bring out existing knowledge to be reshaped by new points of view" (p. 111).

In the first year of the Warren/Maldonado group, Kathy realized that the group was experiencing difficulty with presentational and assessing talk. She brought Barnes's work to share with the group and to have an open discussion about how this talk was affecting the group and allowing some people to dominate while others were silenced. Without "naming names," the group discussed these types of talk and ways to encourage collaboration and exploration.

Silencing also occurs when people hold views that are not shared by the majority of the group. Often this perspective is that of teachers who take a more conservative or traditional approach to teaching. If they do share, two responses tend to dominate. One is to immediately assess that person's comments and to dismiss or judge them as "out-of-date."

The other is to simply accept the comments but not respond or challenge that person in any way. Neither of these responses are productive in the long run. The first silences that individual and often leads to the person dropping from the group. The second does not create a context of growth and learning and can lead to relativism where every idea is considered equally worthy.

Our experience is that the most productive response is to accept and listen to that person's perspective, asking clarifying questions and restating to make sure the group really understands what is being said. Before responding in any way, it's important that the individual feels that the group has listened. In many cases, the individual has taken a big risk by talking about a perspective that is not shared by others in the group. After listening, group members can then share their own perspectives and talk from personal experience about why they believe something different. Their response isn't "You're wrong and here's why" but "In my experience, I've found that . . . "

One of the Warren sessions focused on collaborative curriculum and students asking their own questions. Group members were clearly in support of moving away from more traditional approaches to curriculum and teacher/student relationships. In the midst of this discussion, Bill commented that he had read an article about a Catholic high school that used a traditional approach and was very successful in graduation rates. He stated, "They never ask their students what they want to learn." A member of the group responded by asking him to talk more about the high school, encouraging Bill to extend his comments even though they appeared to be a direct contradiction to the feelings of the rest of the group. As the group continued talking about the high school, they raised questions about how success is measured, ways to support students in asking their own questions, and the role of community support and involvement. By using replying rather than assessing talk, they were able to continue the discussion despite major theoretical differences in their points of view.

In another Warren session, the group talked about moving away from assertive discipline and punishment to having the class develop rules and consequences that fit the broader principles of living in that room. James finally stated, "But five years ago assertive discipline was the district's answer to what was wrong in classrooms and now we are supposed to do this until five years from now when something else comes along and then we'll change our minds." James clearly supported a punishment approach and was taking a risk by sharing this with the rest of the group. Debbie responded by agreeing that there was a problem with the district's assumption that one approach was "right" and then changing its mind. After acknowledging the validity of James's frustrations with changing district requirements, she argued, "Should I do what I believe or do something I'm not comfortable with? This isn't a question for me of what the district wants but what treats kids as human beings." She went on to talk about her own struggles and experiences with classroom discipline.

One exception to this response is individuals who purposely "bait" the group to provoke a heated debate. In those cases, we listen to the comment but then go on with our discussion without responding. We don't ask for clarification or argue because we know from past experiences that the individual really doesn't want to explore the ideas, but instead wants to get people upset.

Does Complaining and Venting Have a Place in Study Groups?

There are times when meetings take on the tone of complaining about problems. These might be problems within the school or district, conflicts with parents and the community, or larger issues involving the state or federal government. Many times these problems are institutional and societal issues that have no easy solution. Group members are frustrated and stressed and the group becomes a place to vent those frustrations.

Some venting is a normal part of the study group. We've all been in situations where having the chance to complain helps us feel better even though the situation hasn't changed at all. However, at a particular point, venting can create a negative tone and take the form of personal attack or gossip about others. In that situation, the best response is to direct the discussion to brainstorming possible short-term and long-term responses to the issue. Participants leave the discussion feeling that some response is possible instead of feeling more discouraged and weighed down with these overwhelming large issues.

In a Maldonado discussion, teachers were upset over the principal's decision that they turn in lesson plans. The group members complained about this requirement and their belief that it didn't fit with their desire to negotiate curriculum with students. The facilitator finally stated, "If we are moving in a new direction, then we need a new model for lesson planning. So how do we share our planning with administration if we are trying to move to a new model of teaching?" This question gave the group a more productive direction for their discussion as they moved to brainstorming other formats for lesson plans.

Warren teachers spent part of one session venting their frustration that the district was mandating approaches to curriculum that were process- and meaning-centered, but then evaluating students' learning on standardized tests that viewed learning as a set of isolated skills. They felt caught between conflicting mandates for changing their teaching and raising test scores. The discussion brought this conflict out into the open, which was important—but the group felt defeated. As facilitator, Kathy encouraged members to brainstorm and think about ways to prepare students for the upcoming standardized tests without resorting to isolated drills. In addition, the group discussed ways to suggest other possibilities for district assessments.

How Do You Deal with Side Conversations?

Another problem that some groups experience is multiple conversations occurring at the same time. Sometimes the discussion becomes so intense that everyone begins talking at the same time. This can be handled fairly easily by the facilitator's getting the attention of the group and saying, "Everyone is talking at once. Let's try and sort out the issues one at a time. Who wants to talk first?"

At other times, the majority of the group is engaged in a discussion while several members quietly have their own conversations. A side comment here or there with a colleague is a natural group behavior. However, sometimes we found that these side conversations occurred continuously and created a context that was disruptive and felt unsafe to other group members, who weren't sure what was being said, and to the speaker, who felt ignored. At Maldonado, the side conversations became so disruptive that the group had a discussion about what was occurring and how to handle it.

In other situations, facilitators have used eye contact with the conversers to get their attention or have invited them to share their opinions related to the issues under discussion. Another factor to consider is arranging the seating so that several people are not sitting behind other group members. The tables should be arranged in circular or rectangular manner so that everyone is in constant eye contact with other members.

How Do Members Come to Value the Dialogue of a Study Group?

One of the most difficult issues we faced in our study groups was coming to value the kind of dialogue that characterizes a study group's explorations. This dialogue was based in developing thoughtfulness as teachers about our beliefs and our practices. It did not produce instant results in that we did not walk away from each meeting with a set of ideas to implement in our classrooms.

For most teachers in our groups, inservices were the only form of professional development they had experienced. The effectiveness of the inservice was judged by whether teachers gained specific information for their classrooms. They saw theory as "pie in the sky" and did not view themselves as theoretical. Theory was something professors did in "ivory towers."

In the study group, we found ourselves spending a lot of time talking around issues and reflecting on what we believed and did in our classrooms. Many initially saw this reflection as a waste of time. They wanted to get right to sharing activities and brainstorming new approaches. They expected the study group to be another inservice, but one in which teachers shared with each other instead of bringing in an outside presenter. They expected to walk away from each meeting with at least one new classroom activity without which they considered the meeting a waste of time. They wanted to "do" things, not reflect on teaching and learning.

While the study group did integrate theory and practice in powerful ways, it was characterized by reflective dialogue, not the presentation of teaching ideas. It took time for us to get to know each other well enough to talk openly and honestly about what we really believed and did in our classrooms. As we analyzed the transcripts from the study groups, we found that it usually took at least a year before the groups were able to really focus their talk and think deeply and critically together. During the first year, the talk tended to jump around from topic to topic and often to skim the surface of a wide range of issues. We believed this occurred because members needed time to get to know each other and to find the topics that would be most productive for prolonged dialogue. While the changes in our dialogue were a natural evolving process, those who wanted instant results were frustrated and not always willing to go through that process. "All the group does is talk," was a frequent complaint.

Over time, we came to value reflection as essential to our role as professionals. Along with Dewey (1938), we realized that action and reflection have to operate in a continuous cycle. Most of us had been so caught up in action that we never had time to reflect. Dewey points out that when we act without reflection, we act on other people's purposes instead of developing our own purposes. However, when reflection has not been part of a teacher's life, it's hard to value the time that reflection takes and to see what reflection adds to teaching. The results aren't instantaneous. We gradually came to realize that we were making more thoughtful decisions in our teaching and weren't as dependent on outside experts to give us new ideas and programs. We got ideas from each other but more importantly we developed a strong base from which to create our own ideas. We were able to articulate what we were doing and why to other educators, parents, and administrators. We felt more in control of our own teaching and not at the mercy of every new trend. Those realizations took time and some teachers were not willing to trust that new insights would eventually emerge from this process of dialogue and reflection.

There were meetings when we discussed practice in very specific terms and created classroom engagements with each other. There were other meetings, however, when we discussed "big" issues like cultural diversity that were based in teachers' perspectives, not on specific engagements for the classroom. We had to come to value these "big" issues because they affected how we thought and interacted with our students, even though we didn't immediately see how those changes in perspective affected our teaching the next day.

We also had to realize that talking about our beliefs *is* theory. Most of us saw theory as educational jargon that had to be referenced to particular theorists, not something we did by reflecting on our beliefs. Our reflections did not seem like important talk because they didn't have a particular "label" or reference.

Confronting these issues is critical to determining whether or not a group continues or dissolves. One important issue is the need to integrate both theory and practice in discussions. As we mentioned in Chapter 1, if we found that our sessions were focusing on sharing activities, we took time to step back and talk about *why* we would do these activities. If we found ourselves heavily engaged in theoretical discussions, we made sure that we also reflected on the ways in which these theories could make a difference in our classrooms—*what* we could do.

It was also important that several times a year we had reflection sessions where we sat back as a group and reflected on the group itself, both the topics we were discussing and the ways in which the group was functioning. These sessions allowed us to openly discuss how this group differed from inservices and what was possible and not possible within a study group format. We saw study groups as part of a larger package of professional development, not a panacea which would meet all needs.

In addition, it became increasingly apparent to us that the summer research teams played an important role in revaluing what the study groups offered to us as professionals. Initially this analysis was only viewed as important for research purposes, but gradually we realized that it was essential to the continuing growth of the groups.

Conclusion

The issues we raised in this chapter are ones we have dealt with in our study groups. Through facing these struggles and making mistakes, we learned how to avoid pitfalls that could have led to frustration and the disintegration of the group. Our responses and strategies may not fit your group and there may be other struggles that your group will encounter. Remember that these problems and struggles are part of human relationships, particularly within a study group context that highlights dialogue and collaborative thinking. They aren't an indication that something is wrong. Our study group sessions weren't wonderful all the time. There were times we weren't sure we wanted to continue, but we did because we found over and over that what we gained from the study group experience was worth the struggle and the times of frustration.

The primary issue that we faced was to create a context that supported dialogue so that members of the group could use talk to think with each other. The following guidelines summarize our insights into ways of talking and listening to each other.

 ## Guidelines for Encouraging Dialogue, Listening, and Communication

Most of the points and examples in these guidelines involve active listening—signaling to other participants that you are listening to them, whether or not you agree, and that you want to understand their perspectives.

Some General Ways to Signal Active Listening

> Use attentive body language as someone speaks.
>
> Focus on what the person is saying rather than your reaction to what the person says.
>
> Try to understand what the person is saying and feeling by putting yourself in that person's place. Try to look at the issue from their perspective for a moment.
>
> Don't immediately offer advice and suggestions or share your own experiences. Take time first to hear the thoughts and feelings and to ask questions to clarify that person's perspective and experience.
>
> Allow people to speak without interruption when possible.

Restating What Someone Else Has Said

Restate the most important points from what someone has said with a question in your voice so that the person can agree or disagree. This gives others a chance to consider what the person has said, acknowledges that person's idea, and gives the chance for clarification.

After restating, check to see if you got it right.

Focus on what the speaker is saying, not on whether or not you agree.

Giving Affirmation to Another Person

Listen for feeling words and check to make sure you understand those feelings. Give the person a chance to clarify how he or she feels.

Empathize:

"You sound really discouraged and tired."

"Are you angry or just discouraged?"

"It is hard."

"I think it's a good practice too."

"It's been a bad week for me too."

"You just needed to think aloud."

Asking Clarifying Questions about What the Person Has Said

Ask open-ended "how" and "what" questions, but avoid "leading" questions such as "Don't you think?" or "Why don't you?" Also avoid questions that interrogate and judge the person and put them on the defensive.

Ask questions for more information or questions that help the person think of other options.

"Can you tell me more about . . . ?"

"What else could have you done?"

"So you're saying . . . ?"

"Why do you think that happened?"

"Is that what you were saying? Did I just say what you said or did you say something different?"

"Why does it bother you?"

Ask open questions, not closed questions with one answer. For example, "How is that important to you?" not "Is that important to you?" Ask, "What were you feeling?" not "Were you angry?"

Referencing Each Other/Acknowledging Another's Voice

Acknowledge other voices by using words such as the following:

"I thought I heard_____offer a suggestion."

"_____brought up an issue last week."

"Going back to your comment,_____, I wonder . . . "

"I'd like to speak to what you are saying."

"I'd like to hook into this."

Inviting Response and Continued Discussion

Use tentative language (maybe, might, could, I wonder) when sharing an idea.

"That might be interesting if we decide as a group that we're all interested in it or we could consider other options. What do you think?"

"What do the rest of you think about this issue? Has that been your experience?"

"What are other issues you've been thinking about?"

Allow short periods of silence to process what is being said.

Offering Alternatives

Here are some ways to phrase suggestions:

"We might tackle this as a whole group or we could meet in smaller groups."

"Well, I was just thinking that maybe . . . "

"I tried a couple of different strategies when that happened to me."

Share what you do so that an alternative is suggested, rather than judging someone else's approach.

Encouraging More Voices

Provide opportunities for everyone in the group to speak.

"Let's spend time and think about it. We've heard from a few people. What do others of you think?"

"It looks like so much is happening in your classroom. Could you talk to us about what you are doing?"

"Do you want to share today?" [Directed at a person]

"What comes to your mind? What are your concerns?"

Challenging but Not Negating or Judging

Here are sample ways in which you could challenge from a positive stance:

"So what was the point of the game?"

"I don't think I understand why you were doing that activity."

A person feels negated and unheard when the next person's comment starts, "But . . . " with a clear indication that the speaker has been rejected instead of first being asked to clarify his or her perspective.

Another way to negate is to tell someone what he or she means instead of restating and asking "Is that what you mean?" Telling assumes you know what the speaker has said and the speaker often feels misinterpreted.

Really listen to the other person; don't use that person's talk time to plan your response.

Strategies for Working through Someone's Specific Issue

Ask many clarifying questions or restate what the person is saying to try and clarify the issue.

Try to get at the broader questions behind the specific question.

Suggest strategies so the person can answer his or her own question, instead of giving answers.

Share an example from your own classroom as one possibility.

Instead of making "you" statements ("You should do this"), make "I" statements ("I've tried this").

Give a suggestion based on what the person is already doing.

Signaling That You Are Feeling under Attack

Clearly state that the issue is of major importance to you and something you are deeply concerned about so that others realize the extent of your feelings.

Make direct statements to let others know how you feel:

"I don't know if you are attacking me or really asking me a question."

"I don't know if you are challenging me or if it's just the way you responded to me."

7 What Is the Influence of Dialogue and Reflection beyond the Study Group?

This chapter grew out of our discussions about the personal as well as school-based influences of the study group. We felt strongly that the dialogue and reflection we experienced within the group influenced our thinking outside the group as well. So we decided to each write individual reflections to share with each other. Through our dialogue, common themes emerged that synthesized why we felt so strongly about the influence of study groups on our own personal growth and on the professional atmosphere of the school. As we talked, the important role that the research group played in supporting the study group process also became clearer. This reflective and analytical role is one that we believe could be essential to a study group's continued existence and productiveness.

This chapter is organized around the questions we asked ourselves in our reflections. The first two sections highlight what we felt were the broader influences of the study group on our personal growth and on school structures and professional relationships. The second half of the chapter describes the research in which we engaged and our reflections on why this research was important to the study group process itself.

What Was the Personal Influence of the Study Group on Us?

Collegial support, a sense of professionalism, and collective thinking provided all of us with a safety net, confidence, and the impetus to continue our own individual professional growth beyond the study group. It invited change with a rich pool of potential ideas, resources, and ongoing tangible support over time for implementing new ideas. "Looking back," Barb reflected, "I realize I was trying more new ideas in various areas, at a greater pace, than at any other time in my career. I gave my students a more active role in their learning because I had a more active role in my learning."

Barb was amazed the first time that someone in the group stated that she didn't know much about a particular topic. "I was afraid to admit I didn't know everything." We found it personally liberating to be part of a group where we could talk about problems and not have to be an expert on all topics. Our reputations as teachers had become tied to "knowing it all" and the study group released us from those pretensions.

Kathleen noted, "I changed my classroom practices to make learning more meaningful. Because I was changing my practices, I needed to talk about my process as I changed. The study group gave me the forum to have such conversations. My biggest change came when I was asked why I was doing this particular practice in the classroom and how it affected students' learning. As I became more involved, I joined other study groups that helped me focus on the process of student learning." Leslie, too, said that it gave her "the chance to change how I taught over time" and to "connect with other teachers."

Through these conversations in the group, Leslie found that she became more articulate about her teaching and was able to talk more confidently and expressively with parents and educators about what she was doing and why. Sandy agreed, saying, "The study group supported me in thinking aloud to find ways to articulate what I was working through professionally."

Clay commented: "It made me a better teacher. It helped me understand change processes, and reinforced my idea to always challenge the status quo." He went on to say that it served "as a reality check on individual perceptions. It helped clarify issues that emerge by looking at more than one perspective."

"Seeing others take risks—helping others take risks," remarked Susan, "was challenging and rewarding, and provided me with a sense of belonging to a community with common goals that I had helped to formulate. It was greatly empowering because for the first time I believed that what I had to say was being heard, acted upon, and made a difference."

Sandy noted, "The study group gave me a place to get information and listen to the rationale for instruction from a theoretical standpoint." She too felt "empowered and better able to trust [herself] regarding attitudes on classroom instruction." She also found she had an interest in furthering her acquisition of "the skills involved in facilitating," and the motivation to take graduate classes at the university. Leslie, Clay, and Kathleen also returned to the university and pursued advanced graduate work.

Kathy learned about working within "a large school bureaucracy," and about "the frustrations of teachers within such a system." She found herself "pushing [her] thinking about the possibilities for change in schools and classrooms and ways of working with people." She had the opportunity to create and experience from within a form of professional development. She thought about "what it means to establish inquiry learning environments for teachers as well as for students. What do we, as educators, need to keep growing and learning?" This thinking influenced how she thought about her courses at the university. "I became more aware of the learning environments I created in my courses and ways to facilitate dialogue so that many perspectives were considered rather than only my perspective. I set up engagements so teachers could experience what we were discussing, rather than only talking *about* that concept or idea."

For all of us, there was a revelation as to the inherent power in facilitation skills and facilitative language to effect change. It was a power that not only transformed adult relationships, creating a professional environment for staff interactions, but it was a skill and an attitude we brought into our classrooms and into our daily lives. As Leslie and Sandy observed, "Facilitation teaches one to listen, to attend to the silent voices, to value people's words, to suspend judgement, to create bridges between children and between thoughts, to create community. Facilitation is a philosophy, a way of being, that permeates our teaching and interactions with children and adults." Above and beyond being teachers, we were facilitators; we were in a position to encourage children to take responsibility for their own learning.

In the study group, we experienced personal empowerment, primarily because the changes we made were a matter of choice, not mandate. Whatever we did, however we did it, in whatever time it took, our choices would be respected.

What Was the Influence of the Study Group on School Structures and Relationships?

Inevitably, a study group influences structures and relationships outside of its immediate arena of activity. On the negative side, if members of the study group fail to establish a low risk environment that respects all points of view, it is possible that cliques of teachers advocating particular positions will form, creating a competitive political environment in the school. And if a particular clique appears to have the ear of the principal, the potential for conflict is greatly exacerbated.

On the other hand, if care is taken to create a nurturing, facilitative atmosphere within the study group where all members feel valued and respected, the potential for schoolwide growth is enormous. The influence of the group spreads out far beyond the actual study group meetings and members to establish a sense of broader collegiality and professionalism in the school.

The themes of community building and schoolwide professional growth were continuously repeated in our reflections on the broader influence of the study group in our schools. Leslie reflected that because of the inquiry in the study group, "It made it possible to visit classrooms and have a sense of what people were teaching without feeling as though I was intruding in someone's 'private' classroom. The school became more connected. I came away thinking that I did not have all the answers and that children learn in a wide variety of ways that can be supported through a variety of teaching strategies."

Kathleen remarked that "people seemed to go out of their way to try and understand each other. If there was a problem or concern of one person, others seemed to rally behind her/him. There was more of a camaraderie among teachers." Susan concurred, "Communication led to understanding, tolerance, and even appreciation of our differences. There was an awareness that we were stronger for those differences. As we shared ideas and became aware of others' areas of expertise, competitive and critical attitudes seemed to self-eliminate. Networks of collaboration and communication became more safe, more honest, and open."

Sandy noted, "The study group set us on the road to unity in the sense that misunderstandings surfaced and were straightened out. Teaching children became more important than personal agendas and talk in the teachers' lounge began to focus on teaching strategies."

Within the context of the study group experience, the need for a more professional and effective language had arisen, a language that was facilitative and inquiring, rather than critical and assertive. The study group created a need for zeroing in on discussion that was meaningful, rather than focusing on personalities; it explored and evaluated theories, asking "how" and "why." This change in language became a critical factor in creating what Clay referred to as an "ethos," a character/identity-defining behavior for the staff.

In her interviews with study group participants, Kathy heard many express the perception that the talk in the hallways and the teachers' lounge changed. This in turn "influenced people who didn't attend the study group because the talk in the building changed. They could listen in on these conversations. They made changes in their teaching even though they weren't part of the group." Talk in staff meetings and teacher inservices changed as faculty members were more at ease with, and more professional in, expressing themselves.

Barb noted that communication between primary and secondary teachers opened up. "The study group made it possible for the *entire* faculty to share ideas." Kathy reiterated this point as she observed that the communication seemed to have contributed to a continuity across grade levels, a continuity that "normally schools work at through rules and regulations."

Through communication and organization, study groups simultaneously afford the opportunity to use materials and human resources more effectively, and to bring innovation more efficiently into the classroom and into the school in general. Clay stated, "The study group was a place for thinking aloud with other concerned professionals about the issues that confront our professional lives."

The study group was also critical in facilitating the integration of new teachers and student teachers into the school community. It afforded them the opportunity to get to know other teachers quickly, in more depth than they could have from casual passing in the hall or quick chats at lunch. They were able to learn about the history of the school, available resources, and the philosophical and methodological spectrum of teaching styles represented at that site. They were invited to reveal themselves and establish relationships that would support them as they defined their place in that community. When Barb joined a new staff that had no study group, she experienced a "void," explaining, "We simply do not know each other. I find myself fumbling around trying to find where things are and how to get things done. It is a slow process which a study group could eliminate."

The tenor and significance of relationships among members of a staff are not lost on students. No matter how well a teacher may believe he or she is portraying professional courtesy toward colleagues, the absence of warmth and ease, and the frequency of cooperative ventures, demonstrations of give-and-take, and enriching interactions translate throughout the school as dysfunction. Teachers who do not cooperate and communicate have difficulty teaching students to cooperate and communicate. Study groups provide a structure and environment within which staff members can learn skills and lay the groundwork for a healthy, communal environment.

Besides the themes of community and professional growth, another theme emerged in our summaries—empowerment. Clay observed, "The study group was a place where people could safely discuss the issues and their initial conceptualization of possible directions with other professionals. It reinforced the idea that the staff of the school was responsible for decisions in and about the school. Lip service is often made for 'empowering the staff to make decisions' but it is rarely put into practice. At Maldonado, the staff took the context they were in and accepted the challenge."

Improved staff interaction is, in and of itself, empowering for all members of a school. It eliminates the obstacles created by fear of what one's colleagues will think of our ideas and actions. We don't have to wonder what they think—we know what they think. Colleagues become sounding boards who help us clarify our ideas and make them more effective. Communication opens up opportunities for support from others who may feel as we do about particular educational issues.

Within the context of the study group where members set their own agenda and have an equal voice, individuals are encouraged to take ownership of their beliefs and translate them into actions. Respect conferred by colleagues enhances respect for oneself and legitimizes our opinions. It encourages us to take risks beyond the "home court." Several voices, unified and committed, have power and influence in situations that one might ordinarily believe to be beyond our sphere of influence. And one success forever changes the perception that our efforts cannot make a difference.

What Was the Role of the Research Analysis Group?

During the first year of the Warren/Maldonado study group Kathy received a grant from the University of Arizona Small Grants Program to fund the collection and analysis of data on the teacher study groups. This research was funded by an Elva Knight Research Grant from the International Reading Association during the second year and by a grant in aid from the Research Foundation of the National Council of Teachers of English the third year. The funding supported audiotaping and transcriptions of the sessions in both study groups for three years. Kathy also interviewed each member of each group at the end of the three years about what they thought was significant for them in the study group experience. The grant funding allowed a research team to meet each summer and to collaboratively determine the research questions and engage in analysis of the transcripts and interviews.

The research team was composed of volunteers from the two study groups. Anyone who was a member of a group was invited to be part of the research team. In addition to the authors of this book, Pamella Sherman was part of the team for two summers and Charlene Klassen for one summer. This team worked collaboratively on all aspects of the analysis from defining the research questions to identifying questions from the data, developing categories, and forming conclusions and implications (Klassen & Short, 1992).

The two primary sources of data were the interviews of the participants and the transcripts of the study group sessions. Those of us in the research group always began the analysis by examining the interviews because we wanted to first consider the perspectives of all the study group members. The same question, "What were the significant aspects of the study group experience for participants?" was always used to examine these interviews. Through analyzing the interviews, we then determined the research questions which would guide our analysis of the transcripts. These questions changed our analysis each year.

In our analysis of the interviews the first year, we agreed on the research question about the significant aspects for participants. We first read the interviews individually to note possible categories. From these, we created a common set of categories that underwent continuous refinement and definition as we worked through a group consensus process of coding the interviews. On the basis of these interviews, we then decided to analyze the transcripts based on two research questions. The first question focused on the concerns and issues raised by teachers exploring a literature-based curriculum. The second question examined the dynamics of the study group process. In their interviews, group members had repeatedly talked about building community and collegiality, and so we focused on the roles that people took within the study group and coded these roles within each transcript.

When we analyzed the interviews from the second year of the two study groups, the interviews included many questions about study groups and their relationship to other forms of professional development as well as to issues of curriculum change. Our emphasis shifted and we asked "What is a study group?" We analyzed the transcripts to determine the essential characteristics of a study group as a form of professional development. We analyzed the interviews based on our question about the significance of the study group and continued to refine the categories from the first year.

In the third summer, we again started with the significance of the study group experience through analyzing the interviews. Because so many teachers had talked about curriculum reform the previous year, we added several questions to the interview about the obstacles and supports for curriculum reform. Many of the teachers raised questions in the interviews about facilitators and about what made some sessions productive and others unproductive. We came to see the facilitator's role in the group as more and more important. In our analysis of the transcripts, we examined the facilitator's talk in the group and identified the factors that contributed to a productive study group session. This focus led us to generate a more in-depth picture of group dynamics and the structures that support dialogue.

We believed that our research methods needed to be based in the same theory of collaborative learning as the study group (Klassen & Short, 1992). Since the study group highlighted the importance of multiple perspectives and dialogue to think through professional issues, so did our research methodology. The intense, critical dialogues that we experienced in our research sessions transformed our understandings of research and of the study group itself.

Changing Our Perspectives through Research

Participating in the summer research teams changed our perspectives on our schools and our roles within our schools. We began to notice how curricular changes influence us in our school communities. We also gained a different perspective on what had occurred in the study groups. We became much more articulate through the thinking and negotiating that occurred within our research sessions. This awareness and experience changed our interactions within the study groups. We were much more aware of group dynamics and ways that we might facilitate what was occurring when the groups became tense or unproductive.

We learned how to research and gained tools for research that we could use in our classrooms. We saw interviews, field notes, and transcripts as significant sources of data that we could collect in our own contexts. We learned how to develop categories from this data and other ways of going about data analysis. We also began to look at other research with a much more critical eye, particularly research done "on" teachers which did not include teachers as active collaborators in the data analysis. Often we found teachers referred to as "they" and their practices and beliefs critiqued but their voices eliminated from the research. The analysis became such a key part of the study group experience that we came to see it as a critical part of the overall process of the study group itself, not just something we did for research purposes.

Through participating in the research group, we realized that before reading the transcripts, we only superficially understood our experience. Susan observed, "The research team taught me the value of processing and that what one feels is happening while in the midst of an experience can be very different when considered in retrospect, and removed from an emotional context. Discussions that are perceived to be rambling or negative by participants, can on reflection be shown to be highly relevant, and ultimately positive." Leslie reflected, "While in a study group, it is hard to realize that conversations have as much depth as they do. By nature, conversations feel casual. By looking back, I could see that our conversations had importance, whether they were about building rapport or educational concerns."

Sandy added, "I learned so much more about what was taking place by studying the transcripts than I did by just listening. I learned to value the growth in teachers. I developed an appreciation for the study group as an effective means of staff development by looking at the changes teachers were making over time. I began to realize what research was all about and developed an appreciation for how research can move the thinking of a field of study."

Kathleen commented that she "began to look at [her] teaching through the eyes of a researcher." It was a revelation we all shared and that was extrapolated beyond the group, into our classrooms where it informed the way we planned and taught. Barb noted that it also changed her relationships with other teachers because the analysis gave her new perspectives on her actions and the ways in which she interacted with others.

And Kathy spoke for all of us when she said, "Those of us who participated in the analysis had an additional benefit because how we listened and interacted in the group changed. We came with a different knowledge base about the group and the interactions and so heard the conversations in very different ways. We could see members assuming specific roles and recognized the significance of group dynamics that we would have missed earlier. We could all use talk to facilitate the conversations in ways we would not have been able to before. We understood group processes and that knowledge allowed us to interact and talk in more thoughtful ways."

Although Kathy had participated in research groups before, this was her first time to actually analyze data with the research participants. Previously she had done an initial analysis of the data and then taken it back to the participants for response. She commented, "It totally changes the analysis. There are so many more perspectives, and people have different background knowledge of the situation or the conversation which leads to a much more complex understanding and interpretation of the data. It led me to question the whole concept of interrater reliability, which is the assumption that different people should be able to take the same data set and categories and be able to sort the data into the same categories. Sometimes we took hours deciding where something should go in terms of a category and we all had different perspectives."

Clay pointed out that the working relationships we formed through the research team gave him a sense of how to collaborate with others in research, speaking, and writing. Leslie has found that she now takes particular expectations for her role as a classroom researcher into new projects with university researchers. These expectations challenge the use of teachers as "informants" rather than true research collaborators.

Teachers and their classrooms have often been the focus of university-led research. The study group encouraged us to examine critical issues ourselves and to look closely at what we were doing. Many of us had held a technician's view of teaching and did not see ourselves as creators of knowledge. Through our experiences in the study group and the research team, we started asking our own questions and actively seeking answers. We realized that we had knowledge we could contribute to the field as we presented at local and national conferences. We became committed to teacher inquiry in our classrooms.

Through teacher research, we were better able to examine what was happening in our classrooms. Kathleen said, "By looking intentionally at questions, I was able to see my students' actions in and out of class through a magnifying lens and could focus my attention." Leslie concurred: "I have understood more about the group of students with whom I conducted teacher research than other groups. By conducting teacher research in my classroom and subsequently writing about it, I uncovered the inner workings of the classroom environment." Sandy found, "When implementing change, I have replaced a sense of success or failure with an attitude that classroom experiences, however exciting or painful, are simply life experiences and primarily data to be processed. What worked? What didn't? What should I retain? What should I abandon?" For some of us, engaging in our own teacher research (Crawford, 1997; Kahn, 1994; Kaser, 1994) was a natural outgrowth of our experiences in the research team.

Analysis and Reflection as a Component in Study Groups

As we stated previously, we initially saw the research group as existing only for the purpose of reporting to the broader field. Over time, we came to believe that this analysis and reflection was integral to the study group process and to the continued survival and development of the study groups.

Kathy observed, "It became clear at the end of the first summer that this analysis was essential to the functioning of the group itself." Sandy added, "It was important in order to develop a procedural format for the group and in defining roles such as that of the facilitator. Reflecting on the group may point out strategies or talk or procedures that were productive and that should be repeated, and also may point out negatives that kept the study group from being as powerful as it had the potential to be. Reflection on the discussions often led to identifying issues that were overlooked that might be interesting to follow, or to seeing that some people showed growth or were silenced."

Barb noted, "The analysis gave us direction on what worked and what didn't work in the study groups." Kathy added, "Without the reflective component, I think the study groups would not have continued at the schools as long as they did." In fact, as Susan commented, "The emotional climate of the Maldonado group at the end of their first year on their own indicated a good deal of discouragement. Sharing the analysis of the transcripts at the beginning of the next year, showing the positive net results, explaining what worked and why things went wrong is what led them to vote in favor of continuing with the study group." Kathy noted, "By reporting what we had seen back to the study group, the group had a way to reinvent itself each year, to revalue what had occurred and see where to go next."

We realize that we had the advantage of special grant funding in order to support this reflection and analysis. This funding gave us the luxury of two to three weeks each summer to intensively focus on the study group process. Because we believe that this component is significant to the study group process, we encourage other study groups to pursue various possibilities for bringing this component into their own groups. School districts often fund special summer curriculum projects and it may be possible to persuade the district that analysis of the study group is a worthwhile week-long project for a group of teachers.

Rather than individual oral interviews, each member might be asked for a written reflection on several key questions at the end of the year. Study group sessions could be taped and several chosen for transcription. Several people from the study group could then examine the written reflections and read through the transcripts to reflect on the group process. A week or even two to three days would provide time for some analysis. If that's not possible, another option might be scheduling a half-day or full-day retreat for the study group during the summer when they can sit back and reflect. They could share their differing perceptions on what worked and hadn't worked and make plans for the following year. There are obviously endless variations to how reflection and analysis might be built into your process. Don't give up if you can't get a large block of time. Even a half-day is better than no reflection at all.

Conclusion

For us, the impact of the study group experience was more profound and far-reaching than we could have imagined. Despite possible inhouse obstacles, a study group does not have to curry favor with everyone, nor enlist broad support; it does not even rely upon convincing others to go along with any one particular program or way of doing things. The study group can be whatever you need it to be. The very fact that our groups have survived for seven years, albeit changing and recreating to stay relevant, speaks to its success and validity as a vehicle for support and growth.

One can never really predict the effects that a certain course of action will have in the long run. As we have discussed, we all had our own reasons for becoming part of a study group. Most of us had modest goals—looking for answers to immediate questions. Over time, we came to share a vision of meaningful and enduring curricular reform through a new approach to professional development.

It is rare to experience an approach to professional development that has the inherent capacity to survive trends, district politics, and "musical chair games" with administrative personnel. A study group has this rare capacity because (1) it does not depend on external agencies to initiate or maintain it; and (2) it does not have to assume responsibility for implementing the vision of remote, uninvested parties. There is no commitment unless those involved in implementing new ideas have a hand in originating the vision, defining the goal, and mapping the course. Practical experience informs and validates the problem-solving, decision-making processes, which in turn generates confidence in those visions and suggests the validity of those goals.

A study group promotes an investigative environment that supports individually directed growth and influences the school community at large. While a study group is not the answer to every question and every problem, it does represent a movement away from divisive and isolating competitiveness, toward synergistic collaborations. It is a seed that can encourage teachers to believe in their right and their ability to ask and investigate questions, and to propose solutions. Through the study group, teachers confer upon themselves the respect often denied by bureaucratic traditions; they affirm themselves the educational experts and acknowledge their own professionalism.

References

Barnes, D. (1976). *From communication to curriculum.* New York: Penguin.

Cochran-Smith, M., & Lytle, S. (1990). Research on teaching and teacher research: The issues that divide. *Educational Researcher, 19,* (2), 2–11.

Crawford, K. (1997). *Negotiating a class focus study within an inquiry based classroom.* Unpublished doctoral dissertation, University of Arizona, Tucson.

Curwin, R. L., & Mendler, A. N. (1988). *Discipline with dignity.* Alexandria, VA: Association for Supervision and Curriculum Development.

Dewey, J. (1938). *Experience and education.* New York: Macmillan.

Fullan, M., & Stiegelbauer, S.(1991). *The new meaning of educational change.* New York: Teachers College Press.

Glickman, C. D. (1993). *Renewing America's schools: A guide for school-based action.* San Francisco: Jossey-Bass.

Heckman, P. (Ed.). (1996). *The courage to change: Stories from successful school reform.* Thousand Oaks, CA: Corwin.

International Reading Association & the National Council of Teachers of English. (1996). *Standards for the English language arts.* Urbana, IL: NCTE.

Kahn, L. (1994). *Mathematics as life: Children's responses to literature.* Unpublished thesis, University of Arizona, Tucson.

Kaser, S. (1994). Creating a learning environment that invites connections. In S. S. Steffey & W. J. Hood (Eds.), *If this is social studies, why isn't it boring?* (pp. 57–72). York, ME: Stenhouse.

Klassen, C., & Short, K. (1992). Collaborative research on teacher study groups: Embracing the complexities. In C. K. Kinzer & D. J. Leu (Eds.), *Literacy research, theory, and practice: Views from many perspectives.* Forty-first yearbook of The National Reading Conference (pp. 341–348). Chicago: National Reading Conference.

Lester, N., & Onore, C. (1990). *Learning change: One school district meets language across the curriculum.* Portsmouth, NH: Boynton/Cook.

Lieberman, A., & Miller, L. (Eds.). (1991). *Staff development for education in the 90's: New demands, new realities, new perspectives.* (2nd ed.). New York: Teachers College.

Lipka, J., & McCarty, T. L. (1994). Changing the culture of schooling: Navajo and Yup'ik cases. *Anthropology & Education Quarterly, 25*(3), 266–284.

Moll, L. (1992). Bilingual classroom studies and community analysis: Some recent trends. *Educational Researcher, 21*(2), 20–24.

NCTE Elementary Section Steering Committee. (1997). *The literate life: Exploring language arts standards within a cycle of learning.* Urbana, IL: NCTE.

Peterson, R. (1992). *Life in a crowded place: Making a learning community.* Ontario, Canada: Scholastic.

Short, K. (1992). "Living the process": Creating a learning community among educators. *Teaching Education, 4*(2), 35–42.

Short, K., Crawford, K., Kahn, L., Kaser, S., Klassen, C., & Sherman, P. (1992). Teacher study groups: Exploring literacy issues through collaborative dialogue. In C. K. Kinzer & D. J. Leu (Eds.), *Literacy research, theory, and practice: Views from many perspectives.* Forty-first yearbook of The National Reading Conference (pp. 367–377). Chicago: National Reading Conference.

Short, K., Schroeder, J., Laird, J., Kauffman, G., Ferguson, M. J., & Crawford, K. M., (Eds.). (1996). *Learning together through inquiry: From Columbus to integrated curriculum.* York, ME: Stenhouse.

Short, K., & Harste, J., with C. Burke. (1996). *Creating classrooms for authors and inquirers* (2nd ed.). Portsmouth, NH: Heinemann.

Smith, F. (1988). *Joining the literacy club: Further essays into education.* Portsmouth, NH: Heinemann.

Authors

Left to right, first row: Leslie Kahn, Sandy Kaser; middle row: Barb Birchak, Kathy Short, Susan Turner; back row: Kathleen Crawford, Clay Connor

Barbara Birchak taught a primary multi-age classroom at Warren Elementary School and currently teaches kindergarten at White Elementary School. She received her B.A. at the University of Arizona and continues to be interested in multi-age contexts and in the possibility of bringing all grade levels together in one classroom.

Clayton Louis Connor taught for the Tucson Unified School District at Maldonado Elementary School and Fort Lowell Elementary School. He is presently an alternative education administrator in Pima County, Arizona. He served in the United States Air Force and attended the University of Arizona and Northern Arizona University. His interests are critical pedagogy, mentoring new teachers, and ensuring educational equity for all students.

Kathleen Marie Crawford received her Ph.D. from the University of Arizona while she was teaching in the Tucson Unified School District at both

Maldonado and Warren Elementary Schools. She now teaches reading/language arts courses in the Department of Curriculum and Instruction at Illinois State University. Her research interests include inquiry-based curriculum and supporting teachers as researchers.

Leslie H. Kahn taught at Warren Elementary School and now teaches an intermediate multi-age classroom at Robins Elementary School in the Tucson Unified School District. She completed her Educational Specialist degree in 1994 from the University of Arizona. She is continuing coursework in mathematics as well as participating in a project exploring the connections between the role of mathematics in the home and at school.

Sandy Kaser taught fifth grade at Warren Elementary School in the Tucson Unified School District. She now teaches an intermediate multi-age class at Robins Elementary School where she conducts classroom research and supports teacher study groups as a means to foster professional growth. She is currently completing a Ph.D. with a focus on children's literature and the forming of identity.

Kathy G. Short teaches courses in children's literature and curriculum in the Department of Language, Reading and Culture at the University of Arizona. She engages in collaborative research and writing with teacher-researchers and continues to explore her interests in inquiry, multiple sign systems, and collaborative learning environments for teachers and students.

Susan Ropp Turner teaches a multi-age 2nd/3rd grade class at Maldonado Elementary School in the Tucson Unified School District. She received her B.A. in English and Elementary Teaching from the University of California at Santa Barbara, and her master's degree in Language, Reading and Culture from the University of Arizona. Her professional interests include curriculum integration, reading strategies, and creative writing.